Bd . 4 . 13

D1492213

London Borough of Richmond upon Thames
Library and Information Services

'BLEST RETREATS'

A HISTORY OF
PRIVATE GARDENS
IN RICHMOND UPON THAMES

B M

DEPARTMENT
OF PRINTS AND
DRAWINGS 1984

Illustrations from William and John Halfpenny,
Rural Architecture in the Chinese Taste, 1755.

© London Borough of Richmond upon Thames 1984

Designed by Tricia Gilroy
Printed by J & P Weldon Limited

FOREWORD

Because there is a great deal of material available about the history of gardens in the area now covered by Richmond upon Thames, it was decided that the history of the <u>royal</u> parks and gardens in the Borough should be treated separately at a later date. However, in a general historical context the non-royal gardens should not be considered in isolation from their royal neighbours whose influence must have been felt. We are therefore particularly grateful to Ray Desmond for setting the scene, with this in mind, in his introduction.

ACKNOWLEDGEMENTS

This publication accompanies an exhibition held at Orleans House Gallery from September 5 to October 14 1984 for which a separate catalogue of exhibits has been produced. The book comprises a group of essays on the historic gardens of this area written by the staff of the Library Service and several outside contributors, without whose ready assistance this publication would not have been possible. The Chief Librarian and Curator would therefore like to acknowledge his grateful thanks to the following:

Julius Bryant, Dr T.H.R. Cashmore, Ray Desmond, Raymond Gill, Gerald Heath, Donald Simpson, Maurice Tomlin and Alan Urwin.

CONTENTS

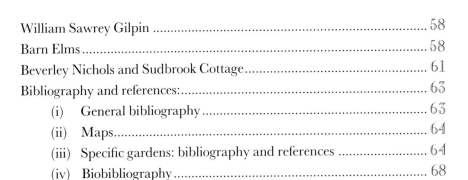

A HISTORICAL INTRODUCTION
by Ray Desmond

For centuries Richmond and Twickenham have been fashionable places in which to live: situated on an attractive stretch of the Thames and not far from London. Henry VII rebuilt his palace at Richmond and his son, Henry VIII, acquired Hampton Court from Cardinal Wolsey. Elegant country villas in spacious parks and gardens inevitably surrounded the royal court.

An examination of state and monastic records reveal that ornamental gardening flourished in this country from as early as the eleventh century. Monasteries cultivated plants mainly for medicinal and culinary purposes and it is not unreasonable to suppose that palaces and larger houses had gardens of a matching splendour.

The mediaeval garden was divided into a number of enclosures planted with herbs, roses and fruit trees; a simple fountain sometimes provided a focal point. By Tudor times the knot garden filled with flowers or coloured earths and gravel had become a popular feature. Wolsey's garden at Hampton Court was representative of its period: geometrical knots, arbours, turf seats and walks. When it passed into the possession of Henry VIII the garden was transformed into a symbol of royal prestige, decorated with heraldic beasts and coats of arms.

The Tudor garden was essentially a series of unrelated compartments whereas its successor in the seventeenth century was a unified whole centred on the house. Sir Francis Bacon who lived at Twickenham Park from 1580 to 1608 expounded his theories of garden design in his celebrated essay, *Of gardens* (1625). He disliked topiary and while accepting contemporary features such as broad walks, low hedges and mounts, stressed the need for diversity and variety in garden design. Mounts for viewing the garden and surrounding countryside were *de rigueur.* Hampton Court boasted a most impressive one, surmounted by an arbour three storeys high. One still survived at Douglas House in Petersham when John Macky was there in 1722; a modest one was included in the recently created period garden behind Kew Palace. Terraces were also popular; the one at Ham House was over 400 feet long. Grottoes, canals and elaborate waterworks reflected the influence of the Italian Renaissance garden. The ambitious plans of the French hydraulic engineer, Salomon de Caus, for Richmond Palace were abandoned on the death of the Prince of Wales. The formal pattern and symmetry of the great Italian and French gardens were sedulously copied. When John Evelyn visited Ham House in 1678 he admired its *'Parterres, Flower Gardens, Orangeries, Groves, Avenues, Courts, Statues, Perspectives, Fountains, Aviaries',* all typical features of the Jacobean garden.

During his exile Charles II became familiar with Le Nôtre's gardens and their grand perspectives and on his return to England had the Long Water and the three radiating avenues of lime-trees created at Hampton Court. William and Mary contributed the elaborate parterres of box scrollwork in the Great Fountain Garden.

Gradually there was a reaction against this geometrical and precise garden lay-out. The statesman, Sir William Temple, favoured the *'artificial rudeness'* of Chinese gardens. For some years Sir William lived at West Sheen where his garden was renowned for its orange trees. His neighbour in adjoining Kew, Sir Henry Capell, also grew oranges and special houses for their cultivation became a sort of status symbol. Wren designed orangeries for Queen Anne at Kensington Palace and Hampton Court; Sir William Chambers included one in his replanning of Princess Augusta's garden at Kew.

The discovery of the dramatic landscape of the Alps on the customary Grand Tour and the revelation of the romantic scenes painted by Claude, the Poussins and Salvator Rosa contributed to the demise of the formal garden. In *The Tatler* and *The Spectator* Joseph Addison argued that a garden should be free of unnecessary constraints. Like Perpendicular Gothic, landscape gardening was an English invention and our international reputation as a nation of gardeners really started with the eighteenth century garden.

In *The Guardian* for 1713 Alexander Pope who was to create a vaguely Rococo garden at Twickenham advocated *'the amiable simplicity of unadorned Nature'.* He postulated that *'all the rules of gardening are reducible to three heads; the contrasts, the management of surprises and the concealment of bounds'.* Through his poetry, his correspondence and his practical advice he exercised a major influence on the new school of gardening. He and Charles Bridgeman, the royal gardener, helped Mrs Howard to plan her garden at Marble Hill.

Bridgeman was a pioneer in this transition from formality to irregularity. He generally restricted straight avenues to the main axis and effectively used the ha-ha or sunken ditch as a concealed boundary. In the royal gardens at Richmond Lodge he deliberately introduced a rural aspect through the inclusion of cultivated fields and serpentine walks.

His contemporary, William Kent, was the protégé of Lord Burlington whose garden at Chiswick House he helped to design. Horace Walpole hailed him as *'the father of modern gardening'* and considered his special contribution to be his perception *'that all nature was a garden'*.

The new creed did not lack disciples. Samuel Molyneux, Secretary to Frederick Prince of Wales, approvingly noted in 1713 that the Earl of Rochester's gardens at Petersham *'endeavour rather to follow than alter nature'*. Batty Langley, the son of a Twickenham gardener, publicized the *'new irregular style of gardening'* in his *New principles of gardening* (1728), convinced there was nothing *'more shocking than a stiff, regular Garden'*.

All the time the range of trees, shrubs and flowers was being enriched by new introductions from abroad. Sir Matthew Decker grew pineapples and plants from India at his home near Richmond Green. The Duke of Argyll whom Horace Walpole dubbed a *'tree-monger'* imported trees from Europe and North America for his garden at Whitton. When he died in 1761 his nephew, Lord Bute, transferred some of the choicest specimens to Princess Augusta's estate at Kew. Mr Vernon, a merchant trading in the Middle East, brought back a weeping willow to plant at Twickenham Park.

The natural landscape garden was largely the creation of painters and poets. James Thomson who lived in Kew Foot Road, promoted its attractions in his poem *The Seasons* (1726-30). Another poet, William Shenstone, sought to inspire a contemplative mood in his garden at The Leasowes in the Midlands by adding memorial urns with apt classical quotations, a Temple of Pan and even a ruined Priory.

When William Kent died in 1748 his mantle passed to 'Capability' Brown who rigorously imposed a formula of undulating lawns, judiciously-placed clumps of trees and serpentine lakes on the English countryside. Existing gardens were ruthlessly transformed. At Richmond Lodge he obliterated Bridgeman's scheme and Kent's whimsical conceits, the Hermitage and Merlin's Cave, but fortunately for us he resisted the temptation to make any major alterations at Hampton Court.

The Brownian landscape was denounced as being monotonous and insipid by Sir William Chambers, the leading exponent of orientalism. He designed a mosque and an Alhambra as well as the Pagoda for Kew Gardens. The vogue for chinoiserie led Lord Radnor to erect a Chinese summer house overlooking the river in his garden at Twickenham.

Chambers's sympathies lay with the emerging Picturesque school whose conflicting debates dominated the closing years of the eighteenth century. The peripatetic William Gilpin, ever in pursuit of the Picturesque in the British landscape, while conceding the *'beauty and even grandeur'* of the Thames at Twickenham lamented that *'it still falls short, in a picturesque light, of a Scottish river with its rough accompaniments'*. Though Humphry Repton, Brown's successor, maintained the traditions of mid 18th century landscape he was nevertheless influenced by aspects of the Picturesque movement. He reintroduced terraces and balustraded walks and planted flower beds near the house.

The Horticultural Society of London (now the Royal Horticultural Society), founded in 1804, also encouraged the return of flowers to the garden. By Victorian times gardening had become more of a craft than an art, with exciting discoveries in the world's flora at its disposal. The Deputy Director of Kew Gardens, Joseph Hooker, returned from a plant collecting expedition in Sikkim with new species of rhododendrons. The publisher, Henry Bohn, had a collection of over 1,000 species of roses in his garden at North End House, Twickenham. Scientific expertise became available to horticulture after the establishment in 1841 of a national botanic garden in the former royal gardens at Kew.

The greenhouse, large and small, now dominated the

garden. The classical orangery had yielded to large glasshouses like Charles Fowler's conservatory at Syon House and Decimus Burton's Palm House and Temperate House at Kew.

The reaction against these conservatories and the Victorian practice of bedding-out plants was led by William Robinson and Gertrude Jekyll who preferred a more natural display of plants. Much of the character of our gardens today is due to their advocacy of wild and woodland gardens, shrub gardens and especially the herbaceous border with its carefully controlled colour harmonies.

Economic considerations may have made our gardens today much smaller but they have not impeded the inventiveness of those who design or cultivate them. The Isabella Plantation in Richmond Park, the Waterhouse plantation in Bushy Park and the garden of the late Beverley Nichols at Ham are impressive testimony that our skills and delight in garden-making have not been lost.

Engraved for The Modern Universal British Traveller.

View of the SEAT of the late DAVID GARRICK Esqr. at Hampton, with a Prospect of the Temple of Shakespeare in the Garden.

A View of the Seat of the late David Garrick Esqr at Hampton. 1779.

The actor David Garrick acquired his property at Hampton from Lacey Primatt in 1754 and lived there until his death in 1779. His elegant villa and riverside garden were depicted in numerous topographical prints, but most delightfully in a series of views by Johan Zoffany, carried out when the painter was staying with the Garricks in the summer of 1762. These views show the newly planted landscaped garden leading down to the river and the undulating lawn and fine trees around his villa which Henrietta Pye described as being *'laid out in the modern taste'*. Garrick was later to commission Robert Adam to design additions for his house but began by asking Capability Brown to lay out his garden[2]. Garrick's friend Doctor Johnson admired it and said *'Ah David, it is the leaving of such places that makes a death bed so terrible'*.

The major feature in all views of Garrick's garden is the graceful little temple to Shakespeare which was put up in 1755. Inside Garrick placed a life size statue of the poet by Louis Francois Roubiliac which was completed in 1758 (now in the British Museum). The architect of the temple is not known. Both Capability Brown and Roubiliac[1] have been suggested as possible designers.

Horace Walpole records a visit in October 1756:

'John and I are just going to Garrick's with a grove of cypresses in our hands, like the Kentish men at the conquest. He has built a temple to his master Shakespear and I am going to adorn the outside since his modesty would not let me decorate it within ...'.

The Roubiliac statue in its niche was joined by other Shakespeare relics over the years and a richly carved chair which may have been designed by Hogarth[3], for the President of the Shakespeare Club and from which Garrick is supposed to have dispensed charity, in the form of money and cake, once a year, to the poor children of Hampton.

But the temple's main use was as a place for Garrick to dine and entertain his friends. As with many of the riverside properties in this area the estate was divided by the Kingston-Staines Turnpike road and Garrick wanted a convenient way to connect the riverside lawn and the Shakespeare temple to this house and garden. Garrick reported to Dr. Johnson that Capability Brown had advised him to make a tunnel under the road rather than build a footbridge. Johnson replied *'David David, what can't be overdone, may be underdone'*. The tunnel with a grotto arch at the south end was completed by 1759.

Never shown in topographical views are the orangery at the back of the villa or the bath-house made from a converted cottage which stood to the west of the Shakespeare Temple. This was provided with fresh water flowing from a spring which used to be near the junction of the present Broad Lane and Uxbridge Road. The garden behind the villa had a large kitchen garden which he extended, including a grapery, a green-house, mushroom sheds and cucumber and melon beds. In 1772 Garrick wrote to Mrs. Sarah Wilmot about the purchase of sheep:

'I want ye sheep upon my land, not for me to feed upon ... I want to make my grass finer than it is, which I am told sheep do and if I can get a good chop into ye Bargain, so much ye better ...'.

After Garrick's death, his widow Eva Marie lived on at Hampton until her death in 1822 at the age of 97. During Garrick's life-time she enjoyed the garden and is said to have planted with her own hands a cypress, a cedar of Lebanon, a tulip tree and a sucker from Shakespeare's mulberry tree. In later life:

'Mrs. Garrick's greatest pride was ... in promenading her picturesque grounds and explaining with enthusiastic delight, the age and date of every tall tree planted by herself and Mr. Garrick'.

Some of Garrick's riverside lawn and the Shakespeare temple survive as a small public garden. In 1923 the lawn and temple were sold and the new owner built a house adjoining the temple. The incongruity of this house was such that it was purchased in 1932 by Hampton Council who demolished it and restored the garden. In 1977 Richmond upon Thames Council commissioned the firm of Donald Insall to repair the temple.

Garrick's Villa was converted into flats in 1922. The grounds were built over in the 1960s and within the select neo-georgian estate lies Garrick's orangery, much altered. The tunnel under the road still exists but has no public access.

The grotto at Hampton Court House before recent restoration.
Reproduced by permission of the Greater London Council.

Almost all the gardens discussed in this work have disappeared. However at Hampton Court House there exists a remarkable survival; a decayed but relatively unaltered 18th century garden. Eileen Harris's recent article in *Country Life*[1] has established its importance and suggests as its designer Thomas Wright of Durham.

Hampton Court House occupies a highly favoured position facing Hampton Court Green and backing on to Bushy Park. The house was built by George Montagu Dunk, 2nd Earl of Halifax for his mistress, the beautiful singer and dancer, Mrs Anna Maria Donaldson in c. 1757. The Earl occupied Bushy House as ranger of Bushy Park. Mrs Donaldson lived at Hampton Court House until the death of the Earl of Halifax in 1771. The Earl left the estate in trust for the benefit of herself and then her daughter Anna-Maria Montagu. For many years following it was left to a succession of noble tenants, including the 12th Earl of Suffolk, the 4th Earl of Sandwich (the one who bequeathed to us a popular form of food), the Countess of Lincoln (Horace Walpole's cousin), Admiral Lord Keith and the 3rd Earl of Kerry. Early in the 19th century the copyhold was purchased by James Campbell, who lived in the house until his death in 1847, when he was succeeded by his son. The estate was enfranchised in 1871 by the then occupier, Mr A.C. Scott and was then sold to Mr M.B. Sampson, the City correspondent of *The Times*. In 1883 Mr Thomas Twining, of the tea and coffee firm bought it for his daughter Augusta, who married a prosperous Swiss-born banker, Mr Auguste de Wette. Between the Wars it was owned by the Gore-Lloyd family, whose interests lay in the tobacco trade. In 1945 it was acquired by the Middlesex County Council as a home for elderly ladies. In 1965 the ownership passed to the Richmond upon Thames Borough Council. The home was vacated in the early 1980s and was then leased to the 'Save the Children' Fund as a home for Vietnamese children.

Thomas Wright of Durham (1711-1786), astronomer and architect was on intimate terms with the Halifax family for whom he worked at Horton in Northamptonshire. The Earl subscribed to his *Universal Architecture, Book I, Six Original Designs of Arbours* (1755) and *Book II, Six Original Designs of Grottos* (1758) and he seems a likely choice of designer for Mrs Donaldson's house and garden. The features in the grounds which date from Lord Halifax's time are mainly gathered around a heart shaped pond originally formed from a gravel pit. At the north west tip of this are the remains of an artificial ruined arch. Opposite stands a grotto, built into a mound with an arched entrance and two side wings. The front resembles the illustration on the title page to Wright's *Designs*. It is built with over-burned lumps of brick, clinker and tufa stone and decorated with large shells, glass, coloured rocks, and bark-covered wood. Inside, the walls and narrow columns flanking the bays are encrusted with shells of all sizes, ammonites and other fossils, coral, quartz and coloured stone. The central bay contains a shell centrepiece. The side bays have small windows which are recorded as having once contained stained glass. The ceiling, now lost, had been painted blue and applied with gilded wooden stars.

East of the grotto, standing on a little wooded mound is an octagonal gothic pavilion built in similar materials as the grotto. Recent investigations have revealed inside, a saucer shaped sub floor of brick. It appears that this building was once an ice house which was then atlered in the early 19th century. The walls up to the roof, which is itself of solid construction, date from the 18th century whereas the additional parapet above, the windows and the fireplace, which has a form of shell decoration resembling that in the grotto, probably date from the time of its conversion into a summerhouse in the early 19th century. It is also thought likely that at this date too, additional work was carried out on the exterior of the grotto, to raise the roof line.

On the northern boundary, against the wall to Bushy Park lies a rocky alcove much overgrown. Urgent repair work has recently been carried out on the grotto and pavilion so that the structures are now sound and weatherproof. It is hoped that the specialised restoration of the shell work in the grotto will be carried out in due course.

Other features in the garden belong to the 19th century. In about 1875 a large conservatory or Palm House was attached to the north west side of the house and was impressive enough to be commented upon and illustrated in both *The Gardeners' Magasine*[2] and *The Garden*[3] of that year:

> 'one of the most remarkable as regards its superior design and finish and the elegant character of the vegetation which adorns it'.

It was stocked with tree ferns as well as palms and other foliage plants. Colour on a small scale was provided by begonias, achimenes, pelagoniums and thunbergias. This glamorous 'winter garden' was designed and built by Messrs. Weeks and Co. The remains can still be seen, a few tall palms, the floor laid with elegant patterned tiles, the highly finished slate borders and a rocky arch; probably the remains of *'a beautiful rockery over which tumbles a cascade … quite a fairy grotto …'*.

An open-work metal arbour known as the Rose Temple within which stands an iron statue (known as 'The Golden Lady') probably date from Sampson's time. To the west of this there was once a rose walk but this part which included the kitchen garden is now separated from the rest and used as nurseries.

WHITTON PARK

Between 1625 and 1633 Henry Saunders, Baliff of the Manor of Isleworth Syon, enclosed several parcels of waste land, totalling about 12 acres, from Hounslow Heath. This estate became known as Whitton Park; it passed through the hands of several owners, was increased to sixteen acres, and in 1722 was purchased by Archibald, Earl of Islay (1682-1761), the powerful politician who became the third Duke of Argyll in 1743. He eventually owned 55 acres in Whitton.

In addition to his political activities, he was a prolific builder and a man of scientific interests, and his main purpose in acquiring his Whitton estate was the cultivation of exotic plants. As Peter Kalm, the Swedish traveller, wrote:

> 'The soil was very meagre, nearly all around being bare ling-heath; but the Duke has been able to show what pleasure, art and money are able to effect, and that by their means the most meagre places are converted into fruitful land'.[1]

He began serious development in 1725, living in a gardener's cottage on the estate until a dwelling was built. The first buildings, began that year, were a 'vollery' or aviary, and a green house; this latter was a very solid building, quite unlike the modern construction associated with the name, and while providing a warm environment for the cultivation of young plants, it also had dining and other rooms. It was designed by James Gibbs. It was not until 1737-38 that a more formal house was built, probably by Roger Morris. Sir John Clerk of Penicuik visited Islay in 1733 and wrote:

> 'he has a fine little canal of about 200 feet in length & about 50 in breadeth. at one end of it is a Large green hous.º ornamented on the outside with Stuco work especially the basse which is rustick. above the green house are 4 or 5 convenient Rooms. at the other end of the canal is an artificial mount with a groto & above a Round Temple supported by two rowes of pillars. the canal is well stor'd with Carp & Tench which thrive wonderfully. behind his green house is a Sort of Court or Area in Grass where he has all manner of conceits & amongst other things some exotick beasts & fouls. on each side of this Area he has pieces of Kitchen grounds & fruit walls. the rest of the ground which seems not to exceed 40 or 50 acres of Land in a kind of natural wood planted by himself. here are several little ponds well stockt with fish & wild ducks & he has Living Springs & rills of water which he brings from the heath which environs the whole'.[2]

The temple on an artificial mount was later replaced by the triangular gothic tower which became a prominent feature of the estate, and whose interior was described in detail by Mrs Pye, who also commented on the *'extensive prospect'* which could be viewed from it. The architect of the tower is unknown, John Adam made a sketch of it in 1748 but both Gibbs and Morris have been suggested as the architect.

The Canal and Gothic Tower in the Garden of His Grace the
Duke of Argyll at Whitton by William Woollett, 1757.

The garden, laid out by Argyll in consultation with his gardener Daniel Craft or Crofts, is shown in the map now in the Bodleian Library. To the west were woodlands intersected by winding paths, and containing fishponds and an aviary; a straight avenue of trees, the Orange Walk, ran through it. Parallel with this was the canal-like pond, with the tower at its southern end. To the north was the green house, with a walled garden behind it containing fish ponds, hotbeds, two glass hothouses, the stables and a long curved wall, heated by stoves, for the growing of citrus fruits. To the east of this complex were fishponds, and south of them was the Roger Morris house; behind it were offices round a courtyard, and in front of it was the bowling green. The whole area was surrounded by a water-filled ditch. Outside the ditch was a nine-acre nursery in the middle of which stood a Chinese summer house surrounded by a fosse wall enclosing a rabbit warren. Here Argyll cultivated the trees and shrubs which were his special interest. The estate was famous for its magnificent cedars, but as Mrs Pye noted:

'In one part of the garden, there is a fine collection of exotics; among which are, the coffee tree, the banana, the chian pepper, the palm tree, the pistachio tree, the torch thistle, and many others, equally valuable for their scarcity and beauty; among the rest, the ever green oak, which flourishes in equal verdure all the year, and has a leaf exactly like the myrtle; also a cork tree.'

In 1765, despite the removal of some of the plants to Kew after the Duke of Argyll's death, some 350 different trees and shrubs on the estate were listed in a sale catalogue.

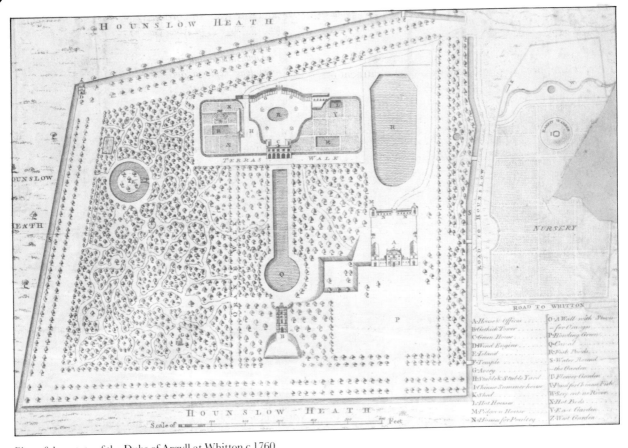

Plan of the estate of the Duke of Argyll at Whitton c 1760
Reproduced by permission of the Bodleian Library.

In 1766 the estate was purchased by George Gostling, a prosperous lawyer, and a few years later he divided it, retaining the green-house, which he enlarged into a substantial mansion, and selling the eastern portion with the house built by Argyll. This was owned from 1781 until his death in 1796 by the distinguished architect Sir William Chambers who made considerable changes on which a contemporary account commented:

'Sir William appears to have had in contemplation the decorations of an Italian Villa. Temples, statues, ruins, and antiques, are interspersed throughout. In one part appears the imitation of an ancient Roman bath; and, in another, a modern temple of Aesculapius, erected in compliment to the Rev. Dr. Willis, to whose skill, under the Divine blessing, we are indebted for the happy restoration of our beloved sovereign to health, in the ever memorable year 1789'.

Another building was a mausoleum, containing a figure of the sleeping Venus and sarcophaguses, medallions, busts and urns *'inscribed to the mightly dead of Greece and Rome'.* Not all observers favoured Chambers' embellishments at Whitton; one paper of 1789 wrote of the grounds as *'crammed with gee-gaws and absurdities … it exactly resembles a Stone-mason's yard, who has left off trade.'*

After Chambers' death, George Gostling Junior repurchased the portion of the estate he had occupied and invited Humphrey Repton to advise on the treatment of the whole estate. Repton's Red Book for Whitton Park contains nine watercolours, but unfortunately its present whereabouts are not known, and a letter from him to George Gostling dated 12 August 1797 contains only preliminary ideas. It seems likely, however, that it was as a result of his advice that the rectangular pond was greatly enlarged into an irregular shape. Gostling later leased the Duke of Argyll's house to Sir Benjamin Hobhouse, but expanded his property in other directions, extending it to some 200 acres. These divisions of the estate led to the somewhat confusing use of 'Whitton Place' to indicate parts of it. In 1847 George Gostling II's son Augustus demolished the house, though retaining the extended green-house. By this time the estate had altered considerably from the ordered symmetry of its original design; a writer in the *Gardeners' Magazine* of 1839 described

> *'the undisturbed state in which the woods appear to have been long kept, in consequence of which some most singular groups of trees have been accidentally formed'.*

Under the ownership of Colonel Charles Gostling-Murray, in the 1870s and 1880s, Whitton Park became a centre for many local activities: fêtes, school treats, sports, and skating on the lake. He died in 1892, and to meet the provisions he had made for his widow, the estate was put on the market. During the following forty years it was gradually whittled away for housing, attempts to save portions for public use meeting with little success. Murray Park is part of the expanded Gostling estate, not the Duke of Argyll's original property. The buildings have all been demolished but a few cedars scattered about Whitton still recall the man whom Walpole somewhat contemptuously categorised as a 'tree-monger'.

KNELLER HALL

Sir Godfrey Kneller (1646-1723) completed his house and garden in about 1711 and lived there until his death in 1723; his widow stayed on until she died in 1729. J. Kip's engraving of the house, garden and park was made in 1715. It shows formal pleasure gardens to the front and sides of the house, with lawns, tree, orchards and kitchen gardens beyond at the back of the house stretching back to Birket's Brook which is not noticeable. We are fortunate in having confirmation of the design of the pleasure gardens near the house shown as a detail by his right arm in his self portrait painted in 1706-11 and now in the National Portrait Gallery.

Rocque's map of 1741 on a much smaller scale seems to indicate that the garden was still there. By the time of Sauthier's map of 1786 the old garden seems to have been replaced by the new naturalism. Birket's Brook which ran through the Park someway beyond the house is shown as a major feature and enlarged into a narrow lake with a long tree lined island. A belt of trees is also shown around most of the perimeter of the Park.

By the middle of the 18th century the estate had been acquired by Sir Samuel Prime. Lady Prime is credited with considerable knowledge of horticulture as recorded in Laetitia Hawkin's *Anecdotes …* (1822):

> *'… but she would have astonished any gardener by her accurate knowledge of fruit and its cultivation. She never made a display even of this knowledge; but a point blank question from my father, who had similar taste, I heard her confess that she believed she knew every pear that grew in England …'.*

But it was Samuel Prime junior who made considerable alterations to the gardens which are described by Ironside as being laid out *'with great judgement and taste to the credit of its owner, and with a liberality of spirit peculiar to himself'*. According to Ironside's description, Prime removed the walls around the house, took down old buildings and *'opened a prospect into Surrey and the adjacent country…'.* Ironside also describes the lake *'over which is thrown a neat wooden bridge'*. A plan of the estate made in 1851 shows the lake with a bridge to the island in the middle still marked. However by this time the property had passed out of private hands and the house virtually rebuilt. In 1857 it became the headquarters of the Royal Military School of Music.

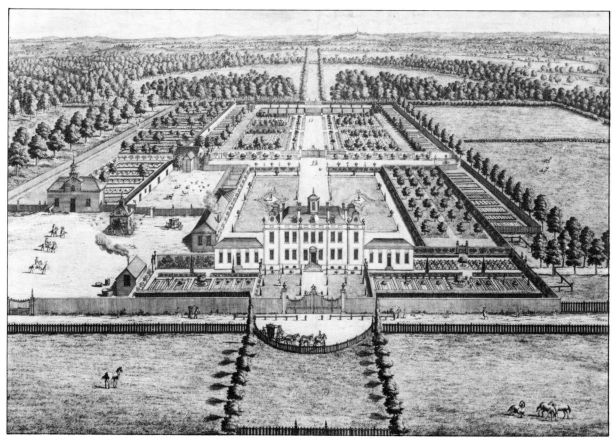

Sir Godfrey Kneller's estate at Whitton by J. Kip, 1715.

South View of Strawberry Hill, 1784.

In 1747 Horace Walpole, seeking a property convenient to London, bought the lease of a small house in an area known as Strawberry Hill Shot from Mrs Chenevix, a toy-shop owner. The following year he bought the house and five acres of land; by his death in 1797 the estate had been expanded to forty-six acres. Soon after taking up residence, Walpole began to extend and transform his house, eventually creating the miniature Gothic castle which still stands.

He also developed the gardens; though at first claiming no skill in the matter, he wrote that he talked

> *'very learnedly with the nurseryman, except that now and then a lettuce run to seed over-turns all my botany, as I have more than once mistaken it for a curious West Indian flowering shrub'.*

He eventually published an *Essay on Modern Gardening* (1785). His *Description of the Villa of Mr Horace Walpole* (1784), however, says virtually nothing of the garden, and the numerous references in his letters are scattered and unsystematic.

In developing his garden, he eschewed the Gothic style of his house; as he wrote to Mann in 1753:

> *'Gothic is merely architecture, and as one has a satisfaction in imprinting the gloomth of abbeys and cathedrals on one's house, so one's garden, on the contrary, is to be nothing but <u>riant</u>, and the gaiety of nature'.*

Nor did he follow the classical symmetry of many formal gardens. In his first years he was particularly active in planting trees. Writing to congratulate a friend on his *'good fortune'* in 1748 he added *'Had it happened to me just now, I believe I should lay it all out in trees'*. A few months later he wrote to Mann:

> *'I have made a vast plantation! Lord Leicester told me t'other day that he heard I would not buy some old china, because I was laying out all my money in trees: "Yes",*

said I, "My Lord, I used to love blue trees, but now I like green ones".

In a letter to Montague he discoursed on various types of trees, commending:

'above all cypresses, which I think are my chief passion; there is nothing so picturesque when they stand two or three in a clump upon a little hillock or rising above low shrubs, and particularly near buildings. There is another bit of picture of which I am fond, and that is, a larch or a spruce fir planted behind a weeping willow, and shooting upwards as the willow depends. I think for courts about a house or winter gardens, almond trees mixed with evergreens, particularly with Scotch firs have a pretty effect ...'.

His love of informality in tree-planting is reflected in the story told of the local nurseryman, Mr Ashe, who said to him *'Yes, Sir, I understand: you would have them hang down poetical'.*

By 1753 he could describe his grounds:

'Directly before it [the castle] *is an open grove through which you can see a field which is bounded by a serpentine wood of all kinds of trees and flowering shrubs and flowers. The lawn before the house is situated on the top of a small hill, from whence to the left you see the town and church of Twickenham ... and a natural terrace on the brow of my hill, with meadows of my own down to the river, commands both extremities'.*

The lawn, the main feature, was both to the east, the direction of the river, and southwards to the fields beyond which lay Little Strawberry Hill. A small walled garden to the west of the round tower contained a circular pool, which he called Po-Yang and in which he kept goldfish, of which he was very fond. He added the lower pond in 1756.

In 1755 he wrote (somewhat prematurely) *'Having done with building and planting, I have taken to farming'.* Ten years later the death of Richard Francklin, the printer, who had been his tenant, enabled him to take over a cottage and garden on the opposite side of the road. Here he built the Bower, a cottage with a tea room and a small library, to which he could retreat from the attention of visitors.

Other features of the grounds were hothouses, two cascades which in heavy rain *'give themselves the airs of cataracts'*, features such as the oak bench designed by Richard Bentley in the shape of a shell, and a few buildings: a little chapel in the wood (still surviving in a very unsylvan setting), the printing press, and the new offices.

Walpole enjoyed his garden throughout his life, particularly in early summer, and his letters include expressions of regret at being detailed elsewhere. Confined to his London house by gout in July 1765 he lamented *'the roses, strawberries and banks of river'*, and in Paris the following year he wrote *'my lilacs pull hard'.* He wrote of *'my passion, lilac-tide'* and of *'the pleasure of lilac, jonquil and hyacinth season'.* In June

'The acacias, which the Arabians have the sense to worship are covered in blossoms, the honeysuckles dangle from every tree in festoons, the syringas are thickets of sweets'.

The songs of nightingales were also a delight, though he wrote in June 1778 of

'the hosts of cuckoos ... It is very disagreeable that the nightingales sing but half a dozen songs, and the other beasts squall for two months altogether'.

The garden of Strawberry Hill has changed more than the lovingly restored house, but though many of the details to which Walpole gave so much time have gone, the stretches of turf and background of trees before the old house recall the main features of his day.

Radnor House, Cross Deep House, Thomas Hudson's Villa, Poulett Lodge

A View of Twickenham by J. Green after J.H. Muntz, 1756
Showing Radnor House, Thomas Hudson's villa, Pope's villa,
Lady Ferrer's summerhouse and Mrs. Backwell's.

In 1756 the Swiss artist J.H. Muntz, who was working for Horace Walpole at Strawberry Hill, made a view of the pretty villas and gardens on either side of Pope's, along that stretch of Twickenham's riverside. Downstream, next to Pope's Villa stood the square, domed summer-house of Lady Ferrers in the grounds of Heath Lane Lodge which stretched to the riverside. However, most of the riverside summer-houses were of a more whimsical nature and in the foreground of Muntz's view, seem primarily to occupy the garden of Radnor House.

John Robartes, 4th Earl of Radnor built his house on the banks of the Thames probably in the 1720s and like Pope united the river and the landward portions of his garden by a tunnel under the road.

Pope wrote scornfully of Radnor, and Walpole christened his house and grounds *'Mabland'*, as the home of fantastic decoration, for he filled the gardens with statues and other embellishments. In 1747 Walpole wrote to George Montagu that *'My Lord Radnor's baby houses lay eggs every day and promise new swarms'* and later in 1754 to Bentley:

'From Mabland I have little news to send you, but that the obelisk is danced from the middle of the rabbit-warren into his neighbour's garden, and he pays a ground rent for looking at it there'.

Mrs Pye, more prosaically, wrote:

'...the garden is not equal in situation to the house, for there is not one view, except that of the river through the subterraneaneous passage, which his lordship cut under the road, for a communication to his garden, from the fine lawn, at the back front of his house, by the river side. But that which surpasses every other beauty, is the cold bath, a small building upon the river, with an alcove at each end; one of which contains the water, and is adorned with the finest shell-work; and a perpetual rill of water drops with an agreeable murmur, in many little streams, into the Bath ... The other alcove contains a sideboard, and the middle is a pretty square room, adorned with pictures: There is also a beautiful Chinese tower, which stands near the water'.

In general the view from the house – *'various beauties ev'ry window yields'* – was admired more than the garden itself, and Thomas Gray thought that Radnor's situation *'far surpasses everything near it'.*

A later occupant of Radnor House was Sir Francis Bassett, and on an autumn day in 1791 Walpole wrote to Mary Berry:

'Hay-carts have been transporting hay-cocks, from a second crop, all the morning, from Sir Francis Bassett's island opposite to my windows. The setting sun and the long autumnal shades enriched the landscape to a Claude Lorrain'.

Radnor House passed through many hands, and in 1846-47 Thomas Chillingworth remodelled it in an Italianate style. Probably in the 1870s, the gardens of Cross Deep House were joined to it. Radnor House and the combined grounds were purchased by Twickenham Urban District Council in 1902, and the 1914-18 War Memorial was erected there. In 1940 a bomb demolished Radnor House; it was not rebuilt, and as some adjoining properties to the north had also suffered air raid damage, the grounds were extended in 1954 up to the wall of Ryan House. In recent years substantial changes in lay-out have been made, including the filling of the channel which separated the island described by Walpole from the rest of the grounds. The small summer-house facing the river is all that remains of the cold-bath; it has been much altered, and the carved wooden entablature was replaced by plain wood in recent years. The main path from the road marks the old boundary of Cross Deep House Gardens, and the Gothic summer house belonging to it also survives.

Adjoining Radnor House grounds were those of Cross Deep House, though the house itself stood on the far side of the road. It was occupied for many years by Stafford Briscoe, goldsmith and silversmith, who died in 1789. Ironside wrote that the gardens *'have ever been noticed for their remarkable neatness and the taste in which they are laid out'* and he also referred to the *'neat Gothic summer-house'* on the lawn.

Between Pope's Villa and Radnor House stood the small villa of the painter Thomas Hudson (1701-79) who retired to Twickenham in 1755. Mrs Pye admired its situation a few years later.

'The back front stands in a lawn of the finest and most verdant turf, close to which runs the river, always smooth, full and clear: on the right hand of the lawn is a little shrubbery, where blooms every fragrant flower and every curious exotic'.

On the landward side of Cross Deep stood an unusual 'Gothick' house on Hudson's land. It is depicted in a drawing by Muntz in which it looks quite like a garden building but was, it seems, another dwelling house and is described by Edward Ironside in 1797 as being the residence of Mr May who was Hudson's nephew and heir. Both houses were demolished at the same time as Pope's Villa in about 1818.

Poulett Lodge stood on the same stretch of riverside nearer to Twickenham town centre. The site is now occupied by Thames Eyot flats. In 1734 William Battie (1704-76) a distinguished physician built his riverside house on the site of an earlier one which had been destroyed by fire. In 1758 it passed to the Poulett family who owned it until 1838. The house and grounds were improved to the designs of F. Chancellor by W.H. Punchard who bought it in 1870. A view of 1879 shows the lawn sloping to a stone balustrade surmounted with vases which can still be seen along the riverside frontage. Gladstone, visiting Grant Duff at York House saw and admired *'that beautiful terraced place'*. It was probably during this period that the loggia of Portland stone which runs up the south western boundary from the riverbank was set up. This leads to a grotto decorated with pebbles, coloured stone and shells and still exists today. The house was used as the Newborough Club in the late 1920s and was demolished a few years later.

POPE'S VILLA

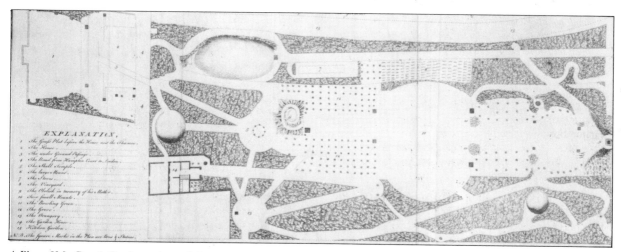

A Plan of Mr. Pope's Garden as it was left at his Death, 1745 by John Serle.

Alexander Pope (1688-1744) was already famous as a poet when, seeking a home which would be healthier and quieter than London, he leased a property on the banks of the Thames at Twickenham. He took up residence in the late winter of 1719 and employed James Gibbs to remodel the house, which stood in the smaller, riverside portion of his estate; the larger portion, of about five acres, was on the landward side of the public highway, and to obtain private access to it Pope had a tunnel – whose entrance is a prominent feature of pictures of his house – built under the road. This he embellished, turning a utilitarian convenience into his famous grotto.

The riverside garden had no specially notable features, being a lawn sloping up to the house, flanked by hedges and trees. A willow which stood in the grounds and which fell in 1801 has been described as planted by Pope, but is not visible in contemporary views of his villa.

Pope encouraged his friends to give him items to adorn his grotto, and in a letter of 1725 to Edward Blount he described it:

'When you shut the doors of this grotto, it becomes on the instant, from a luminous room, a Camera obscura; on the walls of which all the objects of the River, Hills, Woods, and Boats, are forming a moving Picture in their visible Radiations: And when you have a mind to light it up, it affords you a very different Scene: it is finished with

shells interspersed with Pieces of Looking-glass in angular forms; and in the Cieling is a star of the same Material, at which when a Lamp (of an orbicular Figure of thin Alabaster) is hung in the Middle, a thousand pointed Rays glitter and are reflected over the Place. There are connected to this Grotto by a narrower Passage two Porches, with Niches and Seats; one toward the River, of smooth Stones, full of light and open; the other toward the Arch of Trees, rough with Shells, Flints, and Iron Ore. The Bottom is pav'd with simple Pebble, as the adjoining Walk up the Wilderness to the Temple, is to be Cockle-shells, in the natural Taste, agreeing not ill with the little dripping Murmur, and the Aquatic Idea of the whole Place. It wants nothing to compleat it but a good Statue with an inscription, like that beautiful antique one which you know I am so fond of…'.

In 1740 Pope extended and remodelled it, bringing in minerals to give it the appearance of a quarry or a mine.

The garden beyond the road, though small, was developed by Pope with loving care:

'I am as busy in three inches of gardening as any man can be in three-score acres. I fancy myself like the fellow that spent his life in cutting the twelve apostles in a cherry stone. I have a Theatre, an Arcade, a Bowling-green, a Grove, and what not? in a bit of ground that would have been but a plate of sallet to Nebuchadnezzar the first day he was turned to graze' (To Lord Strafford 5 October 1725).

He enlisted the help of friends in developing his ideas, and of one, Lord Peterborough, he wrote in his *Satires and Epistles*:

'And he whose lightning Pierc'd th'Iberian lines,
Now forms my quincunx, and now ranks my vinea;
Or tames the genius of the stubborn plain,
Almost as quickly as he conquer'd Spain'.

Bolingbroke wrote of 'the multiplied scenes of your little garden', and was no doubt referring to the many features which Pope contrived in his limited space. The fullest account is that which appeared in the *Newcastle General Magazine* in January 1748, though the writer 'T' has not been identified.

'Near the Bounds of the Garden, the Trees unite themselves more closely together, and cover the Hedges with a thick Shade, which prevents all prying from without, and preserves the Privacy of the interior Parts. These Wilderness Groves are either Quincunces, or cut thro' by many narrow serpentine Walks; and as we recede from the Boundary and approach towards the Center, the Scene opens and becomes less entangled; the Alleys widen, the Walk grow broader, and either terminate in small green Plots of the finest Turf, or lead to the Shell Temple. The Middle of the Garden approaches nearest to a Lawn or open Green, but is delightfully diversified with Banks and Hillocks; which are entirely cover'd with Thickets of Laurel, Bay, Holly, and many other Evergreens and Shrubs, rising one above another in beautiful Slopes and Inter-mixtures, where Nature freely lays forth the Branches, and disports uncontroul'd; except what may be entirely prun'd for more Decency and Convenience to the surrounding Grass-plots, for no Shear-work or Tonsure is to be found in all the Scene. Towards the South side of the Garden is a Plantation of Vines curiously disposed and dress'd; it adjoins the Wilderness, and is in the same Taste, but opener to the Sun, and with more numerous intervening Paths. Among the Hillocks on the upper Part of the open Area, rises a Mount much higher than the rest, and is composed of more rude and indigested Materials; it is covered with Bushes and Trees of a wilder Growth, and more confused Order, rising as it were out of Clefts of Rocks, and Heaps of rugged and mossy Stones; among which a narrow intricate Path leads in an irregular Spiral to the Top; where is placed a Forest Seat or Chair, that may hold three or four Persons at once, overshaded with the Branches of a spreading Tree. From this Seat we face the Temple, and overlook the various Distribution of the Thickets, Grass-plots, Alleys, Banks, &c. Near this Mount lies the broadest Walk of the Garden, leading from the Center to the uppermost Verge; where, upon the gentle Eminence of a green Bank, stands an Obelisk, erected by Mr Pope to the Memory of his Mother: It is a plain Stone Pillar resting upon a Pedestal; and the Plynth of the Pillar bears this Inscription on its four Sides, beginning with that which faces the Walk.

AH EDITHA!
MATRUM OPTIMA.
MULIERUM AMANTISSIMA.
vale.'

Pope's Grotto by F. Cary after S. Lewis, 1797.

These features can be identified in the *Plan of Mr Pope's Garden* by John Searle, 1745, but unfortunately there is no authentic drawing or engraving of its appearance. William Kent's drawing is obviously whimsical, but is probably reasonably accurate in its portrayal of the shell temple and the arched openings to the walks shown on Searle's plans. There is no doubt that the obelisk (now at Penn House, Amersham) was the focal point of the garden as eventually laid out. Pope was devoted to his mother, who lived with him at Twickenham until her death in 1733. He erected the obelisk in her memory, two years later.

After Pope's death Sir William Stanhope bought the property, enlarged the house and grotto, and made sweeping changes in the garden, of which Walpole wrote in 1760:

'would you believe it, he has cut down the sacred groves themselves! In short, it was a little bit of ground of five acres, enclosed with three lanes, and seeing nothing. Pope had twisted and twirled, and rhymed and harmonized this, till it appeared two or three sweet little lawns opening and opening beyond one another, and the whole surrounded with thick impenetrable woods. Sir William, by advice of his son-in-law, Mr. Ellis, has hacked and hewed these groves wriggled a winding gravel-walk through them with an edging of shrubs, in what they call the common taste, and in short, has desired the three lanes to walk in again – and now is forced to shut them out

again by a wall – for there was not a Muse could walk there but she was spied by every country fellow that went by with a pipe in his mouth'.

The end came when Baroness Howe bought the property in 1807; she demolished the house, stripped the grotto, and further altered the garden. Mary Berry wrote in November 1807

'We went into Pope's back garden, and saw the devastation going on upon his quincunx by its now possessor Baroness Howe'.

In due course Lady Howe's house was demolished and Thomas Young built his curious house to the design of Henry Edward Kendall junior. It still stands, though hemmed in by the more modern buildings of St. Catherine's School; of Pope's house and gardens only the grotto, bereft of its former adornments, survives.

ISAAC SWAINSON'S BOTANIC GARDEN

Mr Swainson lived on the south side of Heath Road in a house later known as Heath Lane Lodge or Heath Lodge (about numbers 87-109 today) formerly Lady Ferrers'. He was the *proprietor of some popular vegetable medicines'* and founded his garden about 1789. Mr Grimwood of Kensington was in charge of the original layout and planting, later succeeded by Mr Arthur Biggs who was later to be in charge of the Cambridge Botanic Garden.

'Scientifically arranged and elegantly laid out, which may be considered as the first private collection of the kind in the kingdom' (Lysons 1811).

J.C. Loudon noted that:

'It contained every tree and shrub that could be procured at the time in British nurseries, and was kept in the first style of order and neatness.' [1]

Ironside added that:

'he was a celebrated cultivator of the vine ... also successfully attentive to the culture of other choice natural and forced fruits and had the finest of every kind of any gentleman in this part of the country'.

After Mr Swainson's death in 1806 the garden was neglected, but after some years Mrs Castles who had known Swainson was given freedom to restore it. It was then described as a ruined

'botanic garden of the old school, combining a Linnaean arrangement with a general disposition of the masses in beds, so as to produce ornamental or picturesque effect ... curious specimens of trees and shrubs, and some good ferns ... 500 or 600 of the commoner (herbaceous) sorts (could still be obtained there) ... there was still a herbarium in good preservation' (Gardener's Magazine, vol. 9, 1833).

This house in Whitton Road, Twickenham was built either just before or just after the Cole family bought it in 1736 with the Brewery, which stood across the River Crane on the present Post Office Sorting Office site. It remained in their possession until 1927. Ironside in 1797 in his *History of Twickenham* described it as

'a neat house, with pleasant garden round it, through which runs a stream of water over which is a neat bridge and under the bridge a small cascade.'

Glover's map of 1635 indicates that the site of Heatham House and the Cole Brewery was previously occupied not by a pleasure garden but by part of the garden and nursery of Vincent Pointer. Gerard in his *Herbal* (1597), wrote:

'many sorts [of pears and apples] are growing in the ground of Master Vincent Pointer a most curious grafter and planter of all manner of rare fruits … the greatest varietie of these rare are to be found …'.

THE MANOR HOUSE, TWICKENHAM

This was situated just a few yards back from the line of Church Street on its northern side. In 1542 it was described as a *'great mansion and garden'*, the first reference to a garden in Twickenham; and in 1547 it was 'the chief messuage in the Manor of Twickenham'.

John Browne, the Clerk of the Parliaments, and a Roundhead, lived here from 1644 until after the Restoration in 1660. After King Charles I's execution Parliament arranged for a survey of royal properties, and the Manor House and its garden comprising 12 acres was included. The report refers to the garden and the park beyond it running up to Amyand Park Road as follows:

'All that Capitall Mancion house Commonly called or knowne by the name of the Mannour house situate lyeinge and beinge in Twickenham neere the Church built with Brick and Covered with Tyle consisting of one Court before the Dore planted with two Mulbery Trees and some Walle fruit Trees … Alsoe one Orchard and Garden lyeinge on the north side of the said hous plentifully planted with Curious and Various sorts of fruite Trees Rootes plants flowers rare to the eye and very pleasant in Tast and profitable for use fitted alsoe with many gravilly Walkes and incompassed about with a Brick Walle … Also one pleasant Large and Longe Walke Lyeinge between the aforesaid garden and the ground called Garretts ground or the Parke lande …'.

There is no plan of this time. However, Glover's map of 1635 shows a small informal garden behind the house and 'a parke' beyond that.

Sauthier's Map of 1786/7 shows a rectangular formal garden now to the west of the house and behind the houses of Church Street on the north side, and the remainder of the park divided into small rectangular plots with no indication of their use. On Thomas Milne's land use map of 1799 all is classified as garden.

There is a plan of the house and garden dated probably 1760[1] and the last that we have in any detail before major disposals of land took place is a plan of the house and garden for the year 1805 which shows a similar layout. It is puzzling that the c.1760 plan shows no formal garden to the west. Most of the remaining 12 acres is intact but now including a number of smaller houses; subdivision and development has begun. Pleasure grounds in front of and behind the house total just over 1 acre, the larger part of the back of the house with trees and a footpath to the east and west sides with the latter stretching back half way towards Amyand Park Road. Of the remainder of the Park there were 5 acres of walled garden and paddock of about 4 acres.

By 1846 the house and 'grounds' only comprised just under 4 acres. In 1863 only the small front garden between the house and Church Street was left.

The Italian fountain and statues in York House Gardens.

Y ork House, one of the principal houses in Twicken- ham has a long history, indeed the name York is first mentioned in a document in 1381. A major house has been on the site certainly since 1635 when Glover's map shows it in scaffolding. The present house dates from this period and from 1690-1700 when further rebuilding took place.

Sauthier's map of 1786/7 indicates lawns both back and front of the house with belts of trees round the whole perimeter of the park except the side facing the river. Ironside confirms this in his *History* (1797),

> *'The lawn before it is extensive; at the bottom of which there is a terrace walk of gravel the whole length of the garden. On one side of the lawn is a grove of elms with serpentine walks* [this was between the house and Syon Row], *and a small summer house from which there is a pleasing view of the river'.*

At that time the garden ended at Riverside Road, beyond which, between it and the river was a meadow where cows grazed in the late 19th Century. This meadow was enclosed with a wall by the Duke of Orleans in about 1897 and the present garden then began to take shape. The Duke also kept a zoo in the grounds. When he sold the property in 1906 to Sir Ratan Tata, the sale catalogue described the grounds as

> *'disposed in spacious lawns, surrounded by fine timber. The side garden is used for an aviary, and there is a Conservatory, with Fernery and Greenhouse, Gardener's Cottage, Potting and Tool sheds. A Rustic Bridge* [it seems to have been of decorated cast iron] *communicates with the Piece of Ground on the Riverside on which is a Tennis Lawn, an Asphalte Tennis Court, a Summerhouse and a Handsome Boathouse* [now the Twickenham Yacht Club] *... This Ground is*

enclosed by a Costly Embankment with Terra-Cotta Balustrading'.

Sir Ratan carried out many improvements to the gardens, principally the creation of the sunken lawn on the riverside of the house, a Dutch Garden now replaced by the car park and the erection of a huge fountain and over life-size statuary at the upstream end of the riverside garden. These extraordinary statues from Italy had been bought in 1904 for Whitaker Wright's Whitley Court, Surrey but never unpacked. Sir Ratan installed them at Twickenham in 1906 and despite repeated attacks by vandals they are still there.

York House is now the Municipal Offices of the London Borough of Richmond upon Thames and the garden is open to the public.

MOUNT LEBANON

Lord Raby (1672-1739) bought a house between Twickenham Ferry and Orleans House in 1701. Raby was the great-nephew of the first Earl of Strafford and the title was revived for him in 1711. During Queen Anne's reign he served on the continent as a diplomat and spent little time at Twickenham. However he improved the house and laid out the garden and it was used by his family, notably his mother, Lady Isabella Wentworth who loved *'Sweet Twitnum'*. She wrote many lively, curiously spelt letters to her son and in 1705 reported to him that the gardens were in good order and the following summer that *'...hear is a vast many graipes, peeches and neckterns and fyne payrs...'*. Many years later Batty Langley recorded and illustrated 'The Wentworth Plumb' *'first planted in the Earl of Strafford's garden... The very best Plumb in England for preserving'* (*Pomona*, 1728). After a hard winter in 1709/10, Isabella's *'fillerys'* (Phillyrea), rosemary and lavender hedges were killed by frost and her neighbour James Johnston lost many plants too. However, *'my youe Trees fflurish mightely and sypres is not dead'*. Her favourite area of the garden seems to have been the Wilderness. In 1707 she described how her page boy *'played of his vyall and sett al the Birds a singin'* there'. She was therefore most distressed in May 1712 when the trees were severely pruned: *'poor Twitnum I could have cryed when I see al the heads of the Trees in the Wildernes cut of'*.

Having improved his property, Lord Raby had a view of it engraved in 1709. This was re-issued two years later when he was created Earl of Strafford. It shows a formal garden with clipped trees and shrubs. Isabella received a copy which had been hand-painted by her son of which she was a little critical: *'I would have had that arch with the twoe doors, into the long walk, dun as it really is, green...'* but she admitted that she found *'altogether its exstreem pretty and the fflower pots upon the wall with greens in them I lyke very much...'*. However Lord Berkeley visiting it from Richmond disapproved of some wooden urns, painted to look like stone set in front of the house *'for it looks too paltry for my Lord Strafford not to afford real stone'*.

To the east of the house, the garden is shown terraced with the arch mentioned by Isabella and also a number of statues. John Macky described the scene in 1722:

> *'His gardens also spacious, but not so much to the Riverside, are adorned with several gilded statues and vases which make a very glaring appearance'.*

This house was passed to the Earl's son William who did not maintain it well and his sister Lady Anne Connoly who inherited it had it pulled down in 1794. A new house was built which became known in the mid 19th century as Mount Lebanon on account of the cedars in its grounds. Eventually the gardens were sold for housing and Lebanon Park built on the land at the turn of the century.

The Earl of Strafford's house (the site of Mount Lebanon), 1711.

The piece of land which was to form most of the Orleans House estate was once part of the Manor of Twickenham and is first recorded as leased out by the Crown in 1567. The earliest account of a dwelling house and garden on the site is found in the Parliamentary survey of Twickenham 1649-50:

> 'Alsoe one square garden lyeinge on the South side of the said house incompassed about with a Bricke Walle comparted Contrived and Converted into severall formes and planted round the Walles with rare Duke and May Cherreyes Vines and Peach with a Gravily Walk with Arbors at each corner leyinge 4 stepps in ascent from the Levell and lyeinge between the Walle and Ballisters and in the middle of the said garden severall borders boarders [sic] planted with rare and Choyce Flowers and with divers small Trees as Cipres Trees and the like and on the north side of the said house one other garden incompassed about with a brick Walle and fitted with Curious and pleasant Gravily Walks plants and flowers of all sorts and kinds not onely Rare for pleasure but exceeding profitable for use alsoe one open Kitchen garden or peice of ground Lyeinge between the River Thames and the first above mencioned garden beinge very plentifully planted with Cabidges Turnipps and Carretts and many other such like Creatures'.

This productive garden was organised in formal compartments, terraced and surrounded by walls and gravel paths. It seems that the kitchen garden was situated on the land between the road and the river, now Orleans Gardens.

In 1671 Mrs Jane Davies acquired the estate. The new occupant was a devout old lady who lived chiefly on herbs and fruit. In 1694 Mrs Davies lent her house to Queen Anne (then Princess of Denmark) and allowed the royal party to pick her cherries.

James Johnston, Secretary of State for Scotland under William III, was the next occupant. Johnston retired from public life in 1702 and 'he amused himself with planting and gardening, in which he was reckoned to have a very good taste'. (Carstare's State Papers)

It seems that making a new garden took priority over the house which was replaced by a new mansion in 1710. However Johnston's neighbour Lady Isabella Wentworth admired his garden in 1705 and in 1707 wrote to her son that Johnston

> 'has [an] aboadenc of men at work in the grownd before his hous, I see six or seven digin; it will be a sweet place when he has don, for I thought it very fyne before'.

Johnston commissioned the architect John James to design his new house. It is interesting that he should have chosen an architect who shared his great interest in gardening. As a fitting tribute to his patron James dedicated his own translation of Dézallier D'Argenville's work *The Theory and Practice of Gardening* (1712).

The earliest known plan of Johnston's estate was made in 1711 by John Erskine, 11th Earl of Mar. At this date the estate consisted of the present Orleans House Gallery grounds, the land by the river (now the recreation ground) and most of Orleans Park School. It shows a formal arrangement with an avenue leading from the house to the northern boundary (along the present Richmond Road), between two rectangular canals. The northern half is flanked by vines and also shown is a feature in the north east corner, probably a mount with an icehouse underneath. In 1714 John Macky called Twickenham 'a Village remarkable for [its] abundance of Curious Seats' and singled out Johnston's as 'much the brightest figure' and describes in the garden a parterre, kitchen garden, pleasure garden, wilderness, grotto, mount and fruit garden where:

> 'he has the best collection of fruit of all sorts of most gentlemen in England. His slopes for vines of which he makes some Hogsheads a year are very particular: and Dr Bradley of the Royal Society who hath wrote so much on Gardening, ranks him amongst the first rate Gardiners in England'.

One of Richard Bradley's books *A General Treatise of Husbandry and Gardening (1725)*, was arranged in chapters according to the months of the year and July is dedicated to Johnston in tribute to 'The many Improvements in Gardens, which have sprung from your excellent Genius…'. Bradley describes in particular, Johnston's skill in planting trees during every season of the year.

Among the illustrations in Batty Langley's *Pomona or Fruit Garden Illustrated* (1728) is a pear called 'Johnston's' dated September 10th 1727. It is tempting to believe that

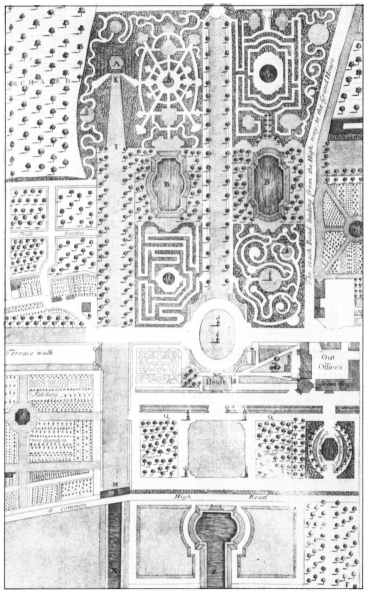

'An improvement of a beautiful Garden at Twickenham…'
(Orleans House) from Batty Langley *The New Principles of Gardening*,
1728 plate IX. Shown in reverse.

the fruit was named after James Johnston and cultivated in his garden, particularly as Batty Langley came from Twickenham.

Langley's 'New Principles of Gardening (1728) includes a plan of an 'Improvement of a Beautiful Garden at Twickenham' which seems to show Johnston's estate. It is depicted in reverse perhaps to prevent easy identification. The central avenue running between the two canals is shown as on the Earl of Mar's plan, as is the Mount, built, Langley says, with earth from the canals for he writes:

'we must dig Fishponds, canals etc. … and with their earth raise pleasant Mounts, Terrace Walks etc. from whence we may enjoy pleasant Views of distant Countries'.

However it is not possible to be sure which other features existed and which are Langley's 'improvements'. From the mount, Langley shows a view down the length of the garden to the river. To avoid interrupting the vista, a ha-ha of water provides a barrier between the road and the garden, rather than railings or a wall. The two canals cut into the riverside portion of the grounds are certainly similarly shown in a drawing by Augustin Heckel dating from shortly after Johnston's death. This shows too, to the east a terraced walled garden planted with small conifers and adjacent, a fruit garden with trees trained against a south facing wall. Johnston's interest in fruit gardening is certainly reflected in Langley's plan which shows fruit trees growing in front of the house and Langley recommends that trees of low growth should be planted so as not to interrupt the view. Whether any of the elaborate labyrinths and mazes existed in Johnston's garden we cannot be sure.

In c 1720 Johnston built an octagonal pavilion in the garden allegedly for the entertainment of Caroline of Ansbach, Princess of Wales with whom Johnston was a great favourite. James Gibbs was commissioned to design the Octagon which is the only part of Johnston's property which still stands. The Octagon was built adjacent to a greenhouse and in 1724 Daniel Defoe recorded that:

'The King [George I] was pleased to dine … in a pleasant room which Mr Johnston built … from whence is a prospect every way into the most delicious gardens'.

Defoe also noted the vines:

'Here is a compleat vineyard, and Mr Johnston who is a master of gardening, perhaps the greatest master now in England, has given a testimony that England notwith-standing the changeable air and uncertain climate will produce most excellent wine …'.

Not everyone paid such compliments to Johnston. His neighbour Alexander Pope mocked his taste by making fun of two little leaden figures of a dog and bitch which stood on one of the high brick walls:

'And Twick'nam such, which fairer scenes enrich
Grots, Statues, urns and Jo--n's Dog and Bitch'.

After Johnston's death in 1737 the property passed to George Morton Pitt and then, by 1764 to Sir George Pocock whose family owned it until the early 19th century.

Known topographical views of Orleans House are always taken from the Surrey bank across the river and so show only the smaller part of the garden by the Thames. Always shown is the copse of trees by the water, west of the house and Octagon. By the 1790s a sloping lawn has replaced Johnston's terraces. However a plan of 1808-12 shows the whole estate which by this time has been enlarged by the purchase of a rectangular plot at the north east end. The mount is still shown and one canal has survived much enlarged and altered to a more pictures-que shape, surrounded by a wooded path and with a grotto in the south east corner. Generally the garden looks more like parkland with scattered trees and an avenue running along the eastern perimeter. There is a large kitchen garden and a melon ground.

Between 1815 and 1817 the house was occupied by its most famous resident, Louis Philippe, Duc d'Orleans who despite being in exile was fond of his Twickenham home and returned to visit it in 1844 when he was King of the French. At this date the house was owned by Alexander Murray who had commissioned the architect John Buonarotti Papworth to carry out alterations to the conservatory which linked the Octagon to the house. In 1850 this was described by W. Keane as

'a beautiful range of glass… gay with camellias of various sorts… the whole embellished with choice climbing plants on arched trellises'.

A carriage drive now swept across the Park from an entrance at the junction of Orleans Road and Richmond

Road, past the mount now referred to as *'a blot on this fair picture'* and the lake, now a neat oval with a fountain. The kitchen garden is much reduced and partially replaced by a wooded area criss-crossed with paths and an Italian walk, a tunnel of vines leading to a grotto. Earl Kilmorey the owner at this time, joined a little island in the river to the mainland forming a headland from which there was a fine view of Richmond Hill.

The gardens of Orleans House were much enjoyed by the next occupants the Duke and Duchess d'Aumale who were greatly involved in local affairs and held fêtes in the grounds. John Dugdale Astley purchased the property and its *'delicious surroundings'*[2] in 1877 and converted it into a sports and social club which was not a success; it was soon sold to William Cunard.

The pleasant woodland garden which now surrounds Orleans House Gallery, a small part of the original estate, was purchased by the Hon. Mrs Ionides in 1926 and bequeathed by her to the Borough of Twickenham. The northern section was sold in 1919 to the Eastern Telegraph Company for use as a sports ground and is now occupied by Orleans Park School.

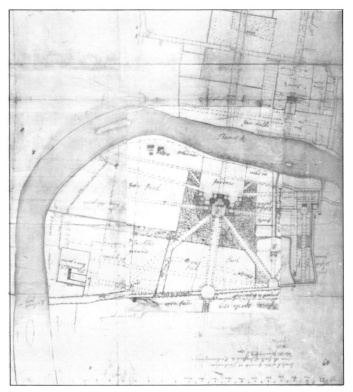

'Scatch of the Grounds at Twitinhame from the Earl of Straffords to Richmond Ferry and also the Grounds of Ham Octob:1711' by John Erskine, 11th Earl of Mar. Showing James Johnston's estate (Orleans House), an unexecuted project on the site of Marble Hill and part of Ham House.
Reproduced with the approval of the Keeper of Records of Scotland.

A view of the Countess of Suffolk's House (Marble Hill)
by J. Mason after A. Heckel, 1749.

Marble Hill House (built 1724-36) is often cited as 'a textbook example' of a Palladian villa, but the grounds are not. This lack of discussion is probably due to the absence of any plans by its designers, Alexander Pope and Charles Bridgeman, that can compare with Colen Campbell's plan and elevation of the house, as published in the third volume of *Vitruvius Britannicus* (1725). But these lawns and trees are important, in their design, in predating William Kent's 'Palladian' work at Chiswick, Rousham and Stowe, in having escaped remodelling in the second half of the eighteenth century in the spirit of 'Capability' Brown, and in having survived the march of bricks and mortar at the turn of the century. The advantages which justify the following brief reconstruction lie in the survival of early bills, correspondence, views and plans that reveal the apparent simplicity of the gardens as they appear today to be deceptive.

There is no marble hill at Marble Hill. The origin of the name is unknown, but must predate a reference of 1350 to *'Mardelhylle'* although the house was known as Marble Hall as early as 1797. The traditional use of the land is indicated by a map of 1711 by John Erskine, 11th Earl of Mar (now in the Scottish Record Office)[2] as meadows, cornfields, fruit and kitchen gardens. Most of the area belonged to the Manor of Isleworth Syon, and was farmed by tenants and subtenants, presumably market gardeners benefiting from soil enriched by periodic flooding.

Archibald Campbell, Earl of Islay, later 3rd Duke of Argyll, was one of the trustees appointed by the Prince of Wales to invest his private allowance to his mistress, Henrietta Howard, later 9th Countess of Suffolk. In 1724 Islay began to acquire land on Lady Suffolk's behalf. Today the estate covers 66½ acres which is more than double the size it was when the house was built, following the purchase by Lord Islay of a total of 25½ acres in 1724.

Charles Bridgeman (c 1680-1738) held the position of Royal Gardener to King George I and King George II and has been called *'the last great gardener to work thoroughly in the French tradition'* of Le Nôtre's Versailles. Little, if anything, reminds us of Versailles at Marble Hill, and were it not for the certain evidence of Bridgeman's involvement, his contribution might be questioned. One reason for this difference may have been the financial deterrents to the French approach of which Bridgeman was well aware having recommended economies to King George II in the year of his appointment. If Bridgeman recommended similar economies to his patron's mistress the only problem lay in keeping costs low without loss of visual effect. Judging from Heckell's engraving of 1749, the main effect was achieved through planting chestnut trees to link the house and river bank. A closer look at this engraving reveals a strict order to the planting which is not simply an arc, but four short parallel rows, each of about six pairs of trees set at right angles to the house and stepped back from the corners of the façade until they reached the river bank. A similar arrangement is contained in the plan for Bridgeman's earliest authentic work, Eastbury in Dorset, the gardens of which he laid out from 1716-20.

The terraces between these trees may be further confirmation of Bridgeman's involvement. They do not appear in Erskine's plan of 1711 and such earthworks would have helped to irrigate and level the soil while serving as flood barriers for the building site. The earliest example of Bridgeman's 'trademark', the *ha-ha* (a trench-like alternative to visible fencing), was dug after 1725 at Stowe, previous to which in 1713 Bridgeman converted the garden terraces there into grass ramps.

Gardeners' accounts reveal the former existence of *'Wilderness Quarters'*, a *'pleasure Ground'*, a *'Sweet Walk'* and ice house, the latter of which still survives.

Alexander Pope (1688-1744) was resident at his celebrated Twickenham villa and garden from 1719, and seems to have become all but caretaker and assistant estate manager to Lord Islay at Marble Hill. No letters or designs have yet come to light that give a specific idea of his influence but one letter written from Sherborne, probably in June 1724, alludes to Lady Suffolk in assuring her friend *'that I have spent many hours here in studying for hers, & in drawing new plans for her'*. Pope described the grounds there with more detail than he ever used for another estate. By 1724 the Digby family had 'naturalized' the seventeenth century gardens in a manner that anticipated Kent's remodelling of Rousham and additions to Stowe by several years. Pope wrote of

'two regular groves of Horse chestnuts, and a Bowling-Green in the mddle of about 180 foot. This is bounded behind with a Canall'.

A bill for work done at Marble Hill by January 1725

includes *'120 ft. of Deal Railling Cross ye Bolling Green'.* A plan recently found at Sherborne confirms this arrangement while indicating a difference between the dense parallel groves and the complex arc of trees at Marble Hill.

Pope's influence might also be traced in the variety of trees as in 1719 he wrote of *'the Paradise of God's own planting, which is expressly said to be planted with all trees'.* Most noteworthy at Marble Hill are the Black Walnut (which is as old as the house) and the tallest Lombardy Poplars in Great Britain.

The most celebrated feature of Pope's garden and the most obvious comparison with Marble Hill was his grotto. In July 1739 Lady Suffolk wrote to her other adviser, Lord Herbert: *'I am at this time over head and ears in shells'* and an account of 1760 records

'an easy Descent down to a very fine Grotto; there is also a smaller grotto, from whence there is a fine view of Richmond Hill'.

The latter has recently been excavated and shells, flints, coral and lumps of coloured glass once used to decorate the walls have been unearthed.

The Gothick 'Priory of St. Hubert' dedicated to the patron saint of hunting, was built about 1758 and described in Richard Bentley's surviving design as *'a farm belonging to the Countess of Suffolk ... built but pulled down after her death'.* The stable clock was built in 1825-7.

To conclude, the grounds at Marble Hill in Lady Suffolk's day were relatively simple in effect. This simplicity at first appears to break with the tradition of French formal gardens with which Bridgeman was associated and also with the 'Palladian' gardens of Pope at Twickenham, Burlington at Chiswick and Cobham at Stowe, almost in anticipation of Capability Brown's picturesque landscape gardens of thirty years later. But this simplicity is only superficial, born from respect for the site, the primary status of Campbell's architecture, and a sense of economy. Perhaps in this light, even without the missing plans, the grounds at Marble Hill may also come to be studied as a 'textbook example' but in a different sense in that they conveniently illustrate no existing definition, but rather invite further research into our understanding of the English Palladian garden.[2]

CAMBRIDGE PARK

Formerly Twickenham Meadows

A house in commodious grounds stood on this site from the early 17th century. For over 130 years it was the home of the Ashe (or Ash) family. In 1751 it was acquired by Richard Owen Cambridge. At the time of his purchase, the house and grounds were much shut in:

'the river, with all the rich scenery on the opposite shore, was so entirely excluded by high walls and terraces, and the ground so crowded and disfigured by numerous avenues and unmeaning masses of wood, that the aspect was the very reverse of ... gaity and cheerfulness'.

By 1760, when Henrietta Pye described the scene, all had changed:

'the meadows are verdant, large and beautifully situated; all along the river side they are level and easy; but higher, the ground rises into little hillocks, and the lofty trees in many parts, offering their shade, render it the most beautiful of places'.

'The grove ... lies not in a strait line but winding in and out; it is covered with a green turf, as soft to the feet as velvet, and fenced on each side by thick bushes of roses, orange-flowers, honey-suckles, lilacs, and sweet-williams, and shaded by fine tall trees. There are many little rustic seats ... [and] the aromatic smell of plants and the warbling of birds ...'.

In Cambridge's day there was a fine row of elms: there in 1760 an anonymous poet left a set of verses which began:

'Ye green hair'd nymph, whom Pan allows
to guard from harm these favoured boughs'

and ended

'Whom virtue and her friends approve
Whom CAMBRIDGE and the Muses love'.

Cambridge continued to live here in *'the hospitable style of a contry gentleman'* until his death in 1802. He was not only a talented amateur gardener but wrote light hearted essays on the subject for *The World* in April 1755: on the *'Advantages of modern Gardening'* and *'Qualifications of a modern Gardener'.* Perhaps it was his stress on the professional experts, who dictated modern taste, which won him the approval of Capability Brown. According to his son, writing in 1803, Richard Owen Cambridge received *'many flattering compliments'* for the layout of his grounds *'particularly from the celebrated Mr Browne'.*

After 1802, the house and its park passed through various hands. In about 1835 it was acquired by Henry Bevan who did much to improve the grounds. The *Garden Magazine* for 1837 noted that there was a *'flat park-like lawn'* of about 60 acres and some *'fine handsome elms'.* Bevan had erected 2 good ranges of forcing houses one nearly 100 ft. in length and had an acre and a half of kitchen garden. In one of the forcing houses, divided into three, there were early and late peaches, and a grapery. Both the forcing houses were heated by hot water, of which the head gardener, Mr Wilson, thoroughly approved. Bevan had also erected an orangery with a hipped roof; the lower portion of the back half being of glass. This also had a central heating system. Finally added to the house on the front facing the river, was a glass conservatory

'well furnished with plants ... ornamental devices and a large vase containing gold fishes ... a handsome appendage to the drawing room ...'.

By the close of the 19th century the old house and its grounds were falling into decay. Parts of the park had been sold off for housing development and the new century saw the development of factories, a bus garage, and an ice rink, alongside the old house. This last was demolished in the 1930s. 'Twickenham Meadows' has now vanished.

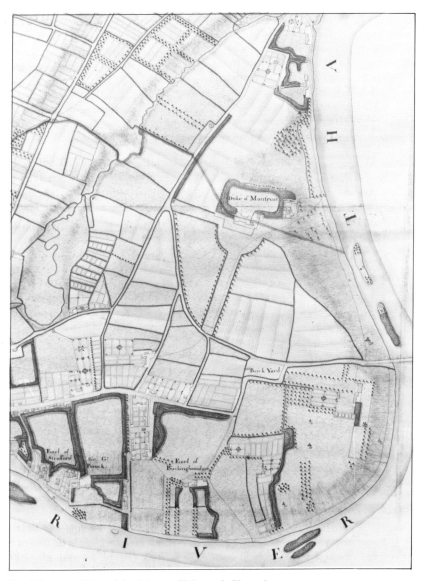

Detail from the 'Map of the Manor of Isleworth-Sion . . .'
by C J Sauthier, 1786/87. Showing the properties east of
Twickenham centre, in particular Marble Hill, Twickenham Park
and Cambridge Park.
His Grace the Duke of Northumberland.

The first major residence in Twickenham Park was built in 1560-1 and it was not until later that Francis Bacon writing to his brother Antony refers to *'that wholesome pleasant lodge and finely designed garden'* but no details have been found. However, in 1608 Bacon sold the Park to Lucy, Countess of Bedford, who built a new house and laid out the first garden in Twickenham that we know about in some detail. The designer is not known, but it seems likely to have been Salomon de Caus, a Huguenot from Normandy who had studied gardens in Italy in the 1590s, and who worked for the Queen, Anne of Denmark, at Richmond Palace and also for Robert Cecil at Hatfield and the Earl of Pembroke at Wilton.

In 1609 Robert Smythson drew a scale plan of Lady Bedford's new house, and also of its formal pleasure garden and kitchen garden.

The formal garden, 280 feet square, had raised mounts, approached by steps, in each corner. These overlooked in the centre of the garden six circles of lime and birch trees, five at twelve and two at eighteen feet spacing, presumably pleached – or trained as espaliers, and with a relatively small central lawn and outside the square of mounts four squares of fruit trees, rosemary, yew *'cut into beasts'* and thorn and quickset.

Glover's map also indicates that in 1635 there was some sort of terrace adjoining the formal garden and opening on to and looking down the length of the lake. This lake is still there within the grounds of the St. Margaret's Estate, and precisely fixes the position of the house.

No detail of the design of the kitchen garden is given on Smythson's plan. It is much smaller than the formal garden, only 135 by 110 feet. However, Glover's 1635 map shows it as having a pleasure garden design rather like the formal garden, and not the rectangular bed design that we associate with kitchen gardens today. *'The layout and design of the kitchen never threw off the yoke of formality'*. In early Stuart times they were designed in imitations of complex knots and parterres; later the layout became simpler although some extraordinarily elaborate designs were conceived. However, it is safe to assume that the majority of kitchen gardens, in practice, were square or rectangular, with beds arranged in an orderly fashion within the overall design, this is the design indicated on Sauthier's map.

Glover's map of 1635 shows the remainder of Twickenham Park with the main features of two main avenues of trees, one stretching from the house (sited in the corner between The Avenue and St. George's Road) towards the river upstream of the present railway bridge, and the second from the house towards the site of Turner's house in Sandycombe Road.

This layout of the garden and the Park continued until some date probably between 1760 and 1786 by which time a more naturalistic arrangement had replaced the old.

We do know, however, that during the ownership of Thomas Vernon between 1702 and 1725 he employed Batty Langley to design some garden features, including trees, or bushes or possibly hedges of hornbeam, in the form of a spiral perhaps 100 feet or more in diameter to mask and improve a large sand pit in the Park to form *'an agreeable and beautiful figure as it now appears'*.

Langley also planted many trees for the Vernons, and in his *A Sure Method of Improving Estates by Plantations...* (1728) he wrote:

> *'I know a chestnut tree now growing on the lands of the late Thomas Vernon Esq at Twickenham in Middlesex whose arms extend full four score feet...'* (p.110)

> *'That pleasant and most delightful seat Twickenham Park hath its beautiful gardens embellished with hedges of hornbeam, which I planted but a few years ago, from the seed beds, as before advised, which by the indefatigable care of the ingenious Mr Henry Timberlin, Gardener to the Honourable Mrs. Vernon of that place are now become very great ornaments to those gardens.'* (p.180)

> *'That most beautiful tree the Roman Platinus of which I planted many in the gardens of the late Thomas Vernon Esq at his seat at Twickenham Park in Middlesex...'* (p.198).

At least three of his Roman Platinus which we now know as the London Plane (first planted in Ely and Barnes in about 1680) are still hale and hearty in the St. Margaret's Lake Grounds with heights of between 98 and 118 feet, and boles of circumference 12 to 15 feet in 1983.

Thomas Vernon is also credited with the introduction of the weeping willow. The 1811 *Transactions of the Linnean Society* record:

'*Mr. Vernon, Turkey merchant at Aleppo, transplanted the weeping-willow from the river Euphrates, brought it with him to England, and planted it at his seat at Twickenham Park, where I saw it growing anno. 1748: this is the original of all the weeping-willows in our gardens*'.

Who the observer was is not known, but a note by the contributor to the *Transactions* says:

'*This is the first authentic account we have had of its introduction; the story of its being raised from a live twig of a fruit-basket, received from Spain by Pope, being only on newspaper authority so late as August 1801*'.

There seems to be no confirmation of this.

The next map or plan of the Park is that of '*...an Actual Survey, corrected and drawn in the year 1786 and 1787 by C.J. Sauthier*'. Clearly the formal and kitchen gardens shown by Smythson and Glover and Tocque have gone, and a more naturalistic style has taken their place. The northern side of the house has a garden enclosed by a rectangular shaped belt of trees. Smaller, possibly kitchen gardens, are shown just to the east of these trees in the area of the out-buildings of the house, and a rather larger formally laid out garden at the northern end of the Park alongside the road to Isleworth and level with Gordon and Lacey Houses and the house later known as St. Margaret's, all on the banks of the river. There is no trace of Batty Langley's 'spiral'. It is odd, however, that the 'pond' or long canal-like lake shown by Glover formed in the time of the monastery and still there today, is not marked. The solution perhaps lies in the silting up process; dredging and clearing out has been regularly done in recent decades. It might only have appeared as a wet ditch in 1786, and been unnoticeable in the landscape of the Park.

After 1805 the Park began to be subdivided and sold, and smaller houses were built, some of which still remain; Willoughby House near Richmond Bridge, Ryde House in Richmond Road and Park Lodge and Bute House in Park Road, Twickenham.

The southern part of the Park nearest the river is shown in a water-colour by J.M.W. Turner, and a print after this of about 1820, both looking towards Richmond Bridge.

The northern half of the Park stretching from the approximate line of the railway stayed as a unit from 1820 until 1851 and was centred on St. Margaret's House which was on the riverside just downstream of the Half Tide Barrier and Footbridge. The estate and gardens here were the work of Lord and Lady Ailsa from 1820 to 1848.

Sir Thomas Rutger writing in *The Gardens Magazine* in 1838 describes his visit here in the autumn of 1838:

'*This place...is situated, also, on the banks of the Thames, from which the lawn is separated by a wall to its level, on which is constructed a substantial iron palisade. In taking a rapid glance through the kitchen-garden, I observed some asparagus pits ... There is a considerable length of wall in this garden. One of the walls is devoted to pears: the trees are fine, and the walls well filled. In the border in front of this wall, a fanciful mode of pear-training is carrying on, by training the trees to circular iron trellises of about 7 ft. in diameter, formed exactly in the shape of an inverted umbrella; the stocks of the trees being about 9 in. high. There being no pines grown here, the forcing-houses are all devoted to peaches, grapes &c., of which there are several ranges, placed in different parts of the garden. At the back of a lawn, the exterior of which forms the section of a circle, stands a plant-house, with two circular ends, projecting in front considerably beyond the line of the centre... At the extremity of the lawn, on the Isleworth side, stands an opaque-roofed green-house, which is now (Oct. 12) furnished by hybrid rhododendrons in large pots. Nothing can exceed the beauty of these plans, as respects their handsome growth and luxuriancy of foliage. One of them, I was given to understand, was purchased at the enormous price of thirty guineas. On the lawn are some of the largest specimens of abele tree that I ever saw, with other trees of inferior note, both with respect to size and ornament. Leaving the front lawn, from which the observatory at Richmond is seen, and proceeding by the walk which leads towards the Twickenham side, we enter the flower-garden, which is laid out with gravel walks,*

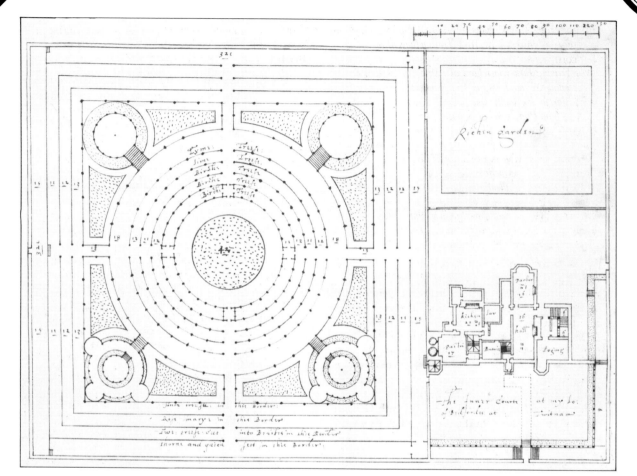

Plan of 'My Lord of Bedfords at Twitnam' (Twickenham Park)
by Robert Smythson, 1609.
The British Architectural Library/RIBA.

but has the flower-beds on grass. At the back of the flower-garden, the shape of which is the segment of a circle, stands the orangery, consisting of a centre and two wings, the centre running back some 30 ft. beyond the back line of the wings. There are some orange trees, with the finest heads I have seen for many years: I counted ten among them, the average of the heads of which was about 10 ft. in diameter; which, as far as I can recollect, is not much exceeded by the far-famed orange trees at Versailles...'.
(*Garden Magazine* Vol. 13, 1838, pp 111/2)

In 1849-50 when Mr Henry Petre was the owner it was described by a visitor:

'From the Gothic Lodge, at the entrance, the carriage-road winds through a park of thirty acres. As there is neither extent nor variety of surface in the park, it is indebted to the trees for all that is interesting in the landscape; but the cedars of Lebanon, horse-chestnuts, and beeches, are of such large dimensions, and of such beautiful forms, that they compensate in a great measure, by their variety of outlines and contrast of foliage, for the want of variety in the ground.

This beautiful ferme ornée, stuccoed, is... encompassed by pleasure grounds of novel and varied character. The ground appears to have been scooped out and raised into high mounds, by which a concave of the most elegant shape, and of pretty considerable dimensions, was formed. This interesting scene of greensward is planted in a manner to represent a Roman amphitheatre, closed at one side by a huge massive wall, begrimed by time, with an archway, when the wild beasts enter from their lairs, and then the sports begin. The area is surrounded by trees to represent spectators ... On one side is a beautiful avenue of lime trees, and on the other is a terrace-walk overlooking the river from which it is divided by a low parapet wall. The north point of this walk is adorned with a temple, in which is a font that was considered of no intrinsic value until it was discovered by William the IV, to be jasper.

On a fine green knole is seated the old chapel of St. Margaret's, inbosomed in wood: and, at a short distance from it, the bright features of a conservatory attract attention and invite aproach. It is fifty feet long by eighteen wide, and contained citron trees with fruit of more than ordinary size, and camellias thickly, but not too thickly, set with flower buds.

The next scene is a range of glass to the S.E. of the house, it is 160 feet long by 25 wide, with a transverse greenhouse attached to the centre 54 feet long and 27 wide.

This horticultural building was formerly the house of protection to the celebrated orange trees that for many years ennobled this place. It is now furnished with a beautiful Atlingia excelsa, fourteen feet high, an Araucaria brasiliana displaying to advantage its pendulous habit of growth, and a large American Aole, indicating, by its rich deep blue colour, a healthy state of growth. In the part now converted into a stove is a large Brugmansia Knightii, covered with a profusion of double white flowers, that perfumed the house.

In front of the range is a large flower garden, the beds and borders are on gravel. The fine broad walks that encompass the beds and communicate with the residence, being a warm colour, harmonize with and give, if we may be allowed the expression, a glow of delight to the surrounding scenery. Adjoining is a study of a different character, but of importance in the elucidation of the fine arts. It is a group of figures by Thom, and represents a scene taken from Burns' Tam O'Shanter...

An avenue of horse-chestnut trees form a noble approach to the archway by which the ampitheatrical grounds are entered. To him the country is indebted for many beautiful seedling verbenas. The following rank amongst the first of that beautiful and useful class: V. Bakerii, St. Margaret's Marchioness of Ailsa, Duchess of Northumberland, Junius, Lady of the Lake, and Lord of the Isles'.

After this, development of this part of the Park also began. In 1854 it largely passed into the hands of the Conservative Land Society who proposed that it be laid out as a garden suburb. This was actually achieved (Ailsa Road, St. George's Road, St. Peter's Road) and it is one of the enclosed grounds that contain the lake, first dug as a drainage ditch in about 1420, and Batty Langley's trees of about 1720.

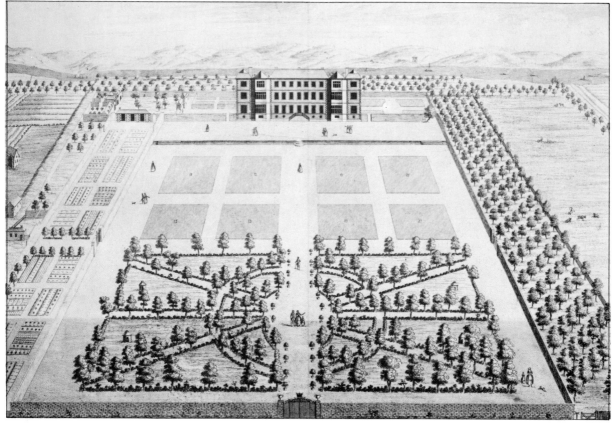

Bird's-eye view of the house and grounds of Ham House, 1739.

A plan by Robert Smythson dating from about 1610 shows that already at that time a strictly formal layout existed, with the house sited on the main axis. Sir Roy Strong comments that this was the earliest example of its kind. The grounds extended in this early period only as far as the edge of the present Wilderness and formed a perfect square, 536 feet each way. The house was approached through the 'Inner Court', on the left of which lay the 'Principall Garden' and on the right, the 'Backe Court' and stables. There was a raised terrace right along the South Front, just as there is today, but it extended at right-angles to enclose the main parterres and orchard which were at a slightly lower level and separated from it by grassy banks with flights of steps at intervals.

In about 1671 an entirely new layout for the now enlarged garden was designed for Elizabeth, Countess of Dysart (who was the following year to marry the Duke of Lauderdale). This plan is attributed to John Slezer, a German military engineer and surveyor, who was also employed by the Duke at his Scottish properties. The new proposals were carried out during the early 1670s, with only slight alterations in some of the details. Like the house, the garden seems to have been neglected in subsequent years, instead of being altered to suit changing fashions as happened so often. *The Richmond and Twickenham Times* commented in March 1884:

> *'Anyone seeing beautiful Ham in the neglected, perishing condition it is in will hear with satisfaction that the young Earl of Dysert [sic] has been warmly advised to take up his abode there in April, and intends doing so. It is hoped that he will transform it . . . to a spot of renovated beauty.'*

In 1948 the house and grounds were given to the National Trust by Elizabeth Dysart's descendents, Sir Lyonel Tollemache, Bt, and his son Mr Cecil Tollemache. In 1975, as a contribution to European Architectural Heritage Year, the Trust decided to restore them by clearing overgrown areas and replanting.

The Main Garden on the South Side

A gravel terrace, with a border of 17th century plants, extends right across the South Front, with steps leading down to eight grass squares divided by gravel paths. The original paths, laid out in 1673, were of gravel dug from Richmond Park, presumably from the Pen Ponds. Large numbers of trees and plants in boxes and pots were listed at Ham in the Lauderdale period, including oranges, lemons, pomegranates and myrtles; these will have been set out round the grass squares in the summer months and kept in the double-glazed orangery during the cold weather. A 1739 engraving shows what appears to be a pedestal for a statue in the middle of each grass plat.

Beyond this area lies the Wilderness. This was a popular feature of late 17th century gardens and consisted of grassy walks in the form of a *patte d'oie*, bordered by trimmed hedges and planted with standard trees. Jane Austen, writing at the beginning of the last century, describes the wilderness at Mansfield Park,

> *'which was a planted wood of about two acres . . . though laid out with too much regularity, was darkness and shade, and natural beauty, compared with the bowling-green and the terrace'.*

The central clearing of the Ham Wilderness was furnished with statues, garden chairs and boxes of shrubs (as can be seen in the painting by Henry Danckerts). The chairs are believed to have been made in the 1630s for use in the house. Chairs of this type had dished seats, so that when they were put out in the garden these naturally collected rainwater; the problem was solved by the joiner, whose bill of 1674 includes an item referring to the chairs, *'for Boring holes . . . for the Passage of the Water'*. The central path through this clearing extends the axis on which the house is sited and continues through the elaborate wrought-iron gates as a formal avenue to Ham Common. The gateways at each side of this garden were erected in 1675-6.

The Cherry Garden

This lies to the east of the house and would have had direct access for the Duchess from her White Closet as well as from the Inner Hall. Its layout of beds criss-crossed by gravel paths can be seen in Slezer's plan. The original cherry trees were presumably trained against the east wall of the garden. In 1679 it was furnished with ten painted garden chairs, a marble statue and flower pots on stone pedestals.

The Kitchen Garden

This lay to the west of the main garden and is now laid out as a rose garden. The Ilex Walk contains one of the original statues, a figure of Bacchus, for which the pedestal, carved with an earl's coronet, was delivered by water in 1672. The low, spreading tree now in the north-east corner is a Christ's Thorn (Paliurus spina-christi), while at the other end of the orangery is a Judas Tree (Cercis silaquastrum).

The Forecourt

The entrance gateway was erected in 1671, to designs of Sir William Bruce, the leading Scottish architect of the time and a cousin of Elizabeth Dysart. The stone was brought by water from Longannet Quarry near the Forth of Firth. As was customary at that time, the gates were painted blue, picked out with gilding. A straight stone path led from the front door to these gates and continued in the form of an avenue leading to a landing stage on the river bank. The forecourt was completely enclosed by walls, broken only by the entrance gateway and round these walls were inserted 38 heads of lead, as they were called in the 1679 inventory. These busts, surfaced to look like stone, portray Roman Emperors and their ladies together with busts of Charles I and II. Twenty-two still remain in the forecourt walls but the rest were resited by the 6th Earl shortly after his succession in 1799, when he took down the front wall and part of the side walls in order

Ham House: The south front and the wilderness, attributed to
Henry Danckerts c.1675.
The Victoria and Albert Museum.

to create the present gravel terrace and ha-ha. The sixteen thereby displaced were inserted in oval niches made in the front of the house, where they remain today. He replaced the straight path with a circular one, of which the statue of a river god forms the central feature. This figure, based on a bronze by John Bacon, R.A., at Somerset House, is made of Coade stone, an artificial stone invented in 1769 and made at Lambeth by the firm of Coade and Sealey. The pineapples he set along the edge of the terrace are also made of Coade stone and variously dated 1799 and 1800. The railings were not added until early this century.

The Ice-House

Concealed among outbuildings and shaded by tall horse-chestnut trees, the ice-house is visible from the upstairs windows of the house. It was built about 1800 and its domed roof of fine brickwork was covered on the outside with concrete during the last war so that it could be used as an air-raid shelter.

In the restoration of the grounds the National Trust have used trees and plants that were available in the 17th century, many of which are definitely known to have been grown at Ham. The Cherry Garden is planted with beds of santolina, edged with dwarf box and surrounded by yew hedges and arbours of hornbeam. Hornbeam has also been used for the hedges in the Wilderness, while the standard trees are field maples. Reproductions of the original chairs and tubs have recently been made and it is planned in due course to furnish the grounds with statues and pot plants once again.

The village of Petersham includes within its boundaries a most unusual number of 'capital messuages' – mansions – with fine gardens. First and foremost is Ham House whose garden is covered separately, but a house demolished in the early part of the nineteenth century had a garden which was, initially at least, of greater importance, this was **New Park** or **Petersham Lodge**. This estate which bordered Star and Garter Hill and the Petersham Road had a difficult site, the house standing on flat ground to the west while the gardens rose 140 ft. above it to the east and were surmounted by Henry VIII's mound, the sole surviving feature of the garden. The building of Lord Rochester's 'delicious house', as Defoe described it, took place in 1692-3 under the supervision of Matthew Banckes. The house was probably designed by Robert Hooke, while the gardens seem to have been the work of George London and Henry Wise (Banckes' son-in-law).

Samuel Molyneux, the resident of Kew House, wrote of his visit to New Park:

'... if Hampton Court did not fill my Expectation the Gardens here I assure you did pay the Pains of my Journey and gave me perfect Satisfaction. I think I have never yet seen any peice of Gardening that has so much as this the true taste of Beauty ... The Partere behind the house and the Hornbeam walks beyond it are well enough but a very high hill to the left of the Gardens part of which is beautifully and wildly dispos'd into Slopes, the rest and upper part cover'd with a fine wood so interspers'd with Vistos & little innumerable private dark walks thro every part of it lin'd on both sides with low hedges with the unconfin'd Prospects you meet every now and then of the Garden below the Country and the River beyond you is what in my opinion makes the Particular & distinguish'd preferable beauty of this place beyond any thing that I have ever seen. I should not forget to tell you that in every walk you meet here and there a little opening in the wood with Seats, a Statue, a grass plott, a Basin of water or the like, for you must know that here is a Fountain playing on the side of the hill (the Spring being at the Top) which is much higher, the Basin of which lyes higher than the house Roof as well as I remember they shew'd us here a huge Cedar of Libanus...'.

The house was destroyed by fire in 1721 and replaced by one designed by Lord Burlington. The new owner was Lord Harrington; he seems to have maintained the gardens for after his death they continued to be praised:

'In the gardens we see simplicity and elegance so blended together, that, like every design of the noble architect art is only used to set off nature, and display its charms in utmost perfection'.

But Rocque's map appears to indicate that by 1745 the layout was already less formal. This tendancy continued through the century, but the gardens during the residence of the Duke of Clarence in the 1790's were still worth noting in *The Beauties of England* (1801-16). The house was demolished shortly afterwards and the gardens reverted to parkland. This property later became known as Petersham Lodge.

The estate lying to the south of the site of the old Petersham Lodge is **Sudbrook Park**. The house was built c.1717-20 for John, 2nd Duke of Argyll by James Gibbs who also worked for John's brother Lord Islay at Whitton. Both brothers had been born and had spent part of their youth at Ham House, the home of their mother's family. Rocque's map of 1741-5 shows that the gardens were of a formal layout interspersed by trees which Islay, a plant collector of major importance, probably assisted in stocking. It has been suggested that Gibbs may have brought in Charles Bridgeman to assist with the planning of this garden as they frequently worked together.

One of the most active gardeners at Sudbrook seems to have been the Duke's youngest daughter, Lady Mary Coke. A glimpse at a year's entries in her journal show that she rarely missed an opportunity to work in the gardens, and reported in 1766 '... the myrtles are in the highest bloom you can imagine'; to celebrate the fact she sent a large nosegay of them to the Prince of Wales. Her work went far beyond the picking of flowers, and her interest was an essentially practical one. Her journal records that she painted the benches, planted and pruned shrubs, spent hours planting and transplanting, supervised the management of the trees marking those that needed cutting down, and saw that 'a good many branches of trees are cut off to open a view to the Hill'. These gardens have, in this century, given way to a golf course.

A near neighbour of Ham House is **Douglas House**

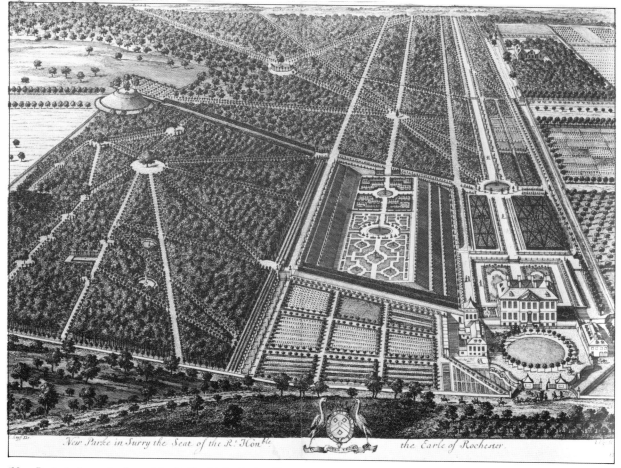

'New Parke in Surry the Seat of the Rt Honbl the Earle of Rochester'
by J. Kip after L. Knyff. 1708.

which was, in the early eighteenth century, the home of Lord Carleton and later of Catherine Hyde (Kitty), Duchess of Queensberry. John Macky found that:

> 'The Lord Carleton ... hath a pretty Seat betwixt Petersham and Ham, with fine gardens: and at the end of his green walk hath erected, upon an artificial mount

[which contained an ice house], *a stately Banqueting-House...*'.

Another feature of the garden was the riverside summer-house which provided a work-space for Kitty's protegé John Gay; the site of this is now part of the Petersham Lodge, River Lane grounds.

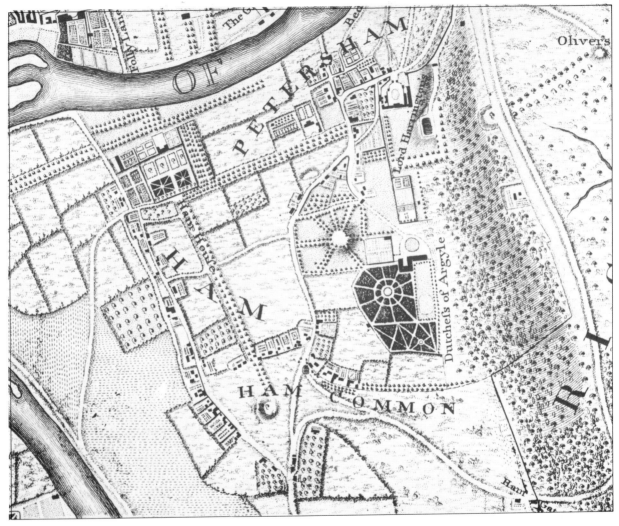

Petersham, detail from Jean Rocque's map, 1746.

Before the end of the eighteenth century another group of gardens had begun to be formed on the slope of Richmond Hill. This land had been used for many generations as a tile or brick works. The clay deposits on the steeply rising ground provided the raw materials for the tile kilns which stood by the Lower or Petersham Road.

In 1765 the Reverend Dr Cutts Barton began his systematic acquisition of the lands and houses on this part of Richmond Hill. Barton was acquiring this property on behalf of his patron the Duke of Montagu. Montagu (formerly George Brudenell, 4th Earl of Cardigan) was by 1743 occupying a relatively small house on the riverside. In 1760 he moved into its neighbour which Henrietta Pye describes:

'The Earl of Cardigan's small house is under Richmond Hill, and stands so shady, that every apartment in it is as cool and as glossy as a grotto. Its pendant gardens are almost in the river, and so thickly planted with trees, that the sun has no admittance'.

Soon Montagu was to move yet again into a new house on an adjacent riverside site. Lady Mary Coke visited it on 6 August 1769:

'I . . . came into the room that looks upon the river with great trees close to it, that protect it from the sun, nothing could be pleasanter on such a day . . . The Duchess of Montagu seem'd in spirits and was very agreeable, the garden they are making upon the Hill will be very pretty but is extremely expensive, as all the ground is supported by timber, and two different sorts of soils are brought to lay over the natural one which is clay.'

Little is recorded about the Duke's work on the gardens, but it is known that the Adam brothers designed a garden-seat or summer house for him, incorporating antique capitals and within an antique pedestal and vase.

Shortly after the Duke's death Horace Walpole and Mr Lysons visited the house:

'The new garden that clambers up the hill is delightful and disposed with admirable taste and variety. It is perfectly screened from human eyes . . . and you climb till at last . . . you recover the Thames and all the world at a little distance'. (Walpole to Mary Berry 29 July 1790)

Daniel Lysons recorded his impressions in *Environs of London, Surrey* (1796):

'At the foot of the hill the Duke of Buccleugh has a villa, which he inherited from the late Duke of Montagu. It is situated on the banks of the Thames. From the lawn there is a subterraneous communication with the gardens and shrubberies on the opposite side of the road, which extend almost to the summit of the hill. They are laid out with taste, and have local advantages superior to most places of the kind in the kingdom.'

Henry Scott, 3rd Duke of Buccleuch had acquired the property through his marriage to Montagu's daughter Elizabeth. In 1819 Buccleuch's grandson inherited the Richmond estate on the death of his mother and it was to remain in his possession until 1884. During this period he acquired the **Lansdowne House** estate, demolished the mansion and incorporated the gardens into his own, thus creating the Terrace Gardens which were to be acquired by the Vestry and opened to the public on 23 Mary 1887.

Lansdowne House had, from the 1770s, belonged to a succession of noblemen including the Earl of Sefton, George, 2nd Marquis of Townshend, Lord Wellesley (Wellington's elder brother) and from 1830 the Marquis of Lansdowne whose principal residence at Bowood had and has a particularly fine garden.

The last of the properties out of whose land the present Terrace Gardens was formed was Lansdowne House's northern neighbour **Cardigan House**, which was built in the 1790s, on part of the Richmond Wells land, by James, 6th Earl of Cardigan. The Richmond guide books of the time make particular note of Cardigan House's beautiful pleasure gardens with their magnificent growth of widely branching trees.

Buccleuch House and its riverside gardens survived as a private estate, although no longer in the possession of the Buccleuchs, until 1937 when it too was acquired by the Council. The mansion was demolished and the gardens opened to the public.

From the mid-seventeenth century to the late nineteenth century residents of Richmond had these series of fine gardens as examples; the sale catalogues show that most of the larger houses had well-maintained pleasure gardens.

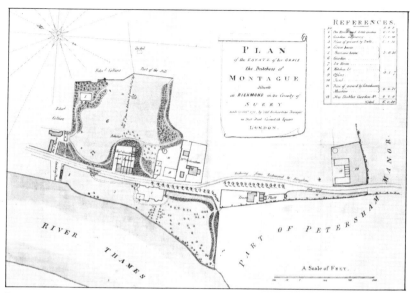

Richmond Hill: Plan of Duchess of Montague's estate, 1771.

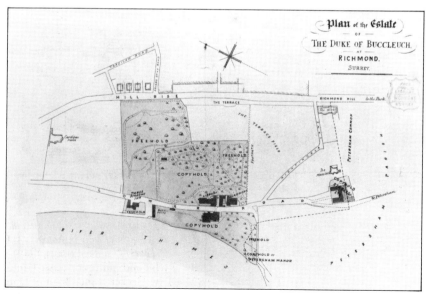

Richmond Hill: Plan of Duke of Buccleuch's estate, c.1906.

A Pineapple: Illustration for the account of Sir Matthew Decker's Garden
in R. Bradley, *A General Treatise of Husbandry and Gardening*, 1725.

L and on the north-west side of Richmond Green was acquired by Sir Charles Hedges (d.1714), the diplomat and politician, in 1690. On this site he erected a large house and developed the gardens which probably incorporated part of the old palace gardens. Not a great deal is known about his works here but we are told '*In the gardens, besides several other curiosities, there is one of the largest and highest hedges of holly in Europe*'. (J. Grove, *History of the Life and Times of Cardinal Wolsey*, 1742). On Hedges's death his Richmond property passed into the hands of Sir Matthew Decker, a merchant of Dutch origin, who had married into the Pembroke family. Within ten years

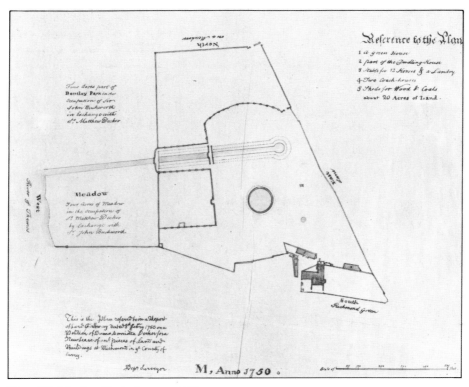

Plan of Sir Matthew Decker's estate, 1750.

Decker's gardens were attracting considerable attention:

> 'The longest, largest, and highest Hedge of Holly I ever saw, is in this garden, with several other Hedges of Ever-Greens, Vistos cut through Woods, Grottos, with Fountains, a fine Canal running up from the River. His Duckery, which is an oval Pond brick's round, and his pretty Summer-House by it to drink a Bottle, his Stove-Houses, which are always kept in an equal heat for his Citrons, and other Indian plants, with Gardeners brought from foreign Countries to manage them, are very curious and entertaining.' (Macky 1722)

About the same time Richard Bradley in *A General Treatise of Husbandry and Gardening* for the Month of July 1725, was writing:

> 'Tis not long since I was Eye-witness to several fruited Pine Apples at Sir Matthew Decker's, at Richmond, about Forty in number; some ripening, and others in a promising condition; the least of which Fruit was above four inches long, and some were as large as any I have seen brought from the West Indies . . .'.

The real achievement belonged to Decker's gardener Henry Telende who put the plants into a brick-lined pit filled with hot dung and tanner's bark and covered it with glass. This hot-bed made in February, lasted through until October. The first pineapple was commemorated in a painting by Theodore Netscher which is in the Founder's Collection in the Fitzwilliam Museum; Lord Fitzwilliam, Decker's grandson, inherited the Richmond property from his mother.

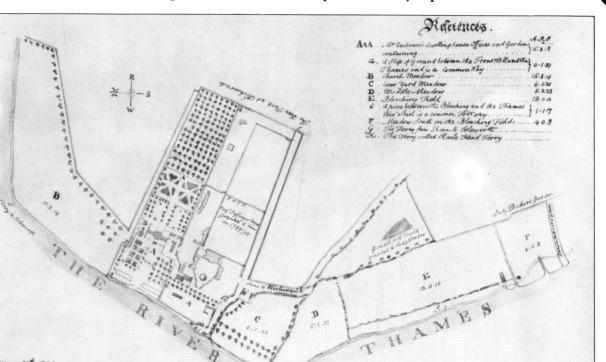

Plan of estates at West Sheen, 1759. Showing the sites of the garden
of Henry Brounker (north) and Sir William Temple (south).

In 1651 Philip Sydney, Lord L'Isle, acquired the old Charterhouse site in the Old Deer Park. Nine years later, after the Restoration, he obtained a further lease of 60 years and commenced the task of turning the property into the seventeenth century equivalent of one of today's 'exclusive' housing developments.

To the north stood the house (built c.1662) occupied in turn by Henry Brounker, Sir Charles Littleton and the Buckworth family. John Evelyn noted on a visit to Brounker in 1678 that *within this ample enclosure are pretty villas and fine gardens of the most excellent fruits'*. He visited the house again ten years later, after it had been inherited by

Sir Charles Littleton; he again comments that *'it is a pretty place, fine gardens and well planted'*. This residence was however overshadowed by the property that lay to the south which initially Lord L'Isle had retained for his own use. Over the next ten years he leased a total of five houses, of varying size, to his friend of long standing Sir William Temple (1628-1699). Temple and L'Isle both had links with Penshurst: L'Isle a son of the great house, Temple at the rectory in the care of his uncle. Both were to go on to take up political careers in Ireland and in 1655 they became neighbours at West Sheen. Two years after acquiring his house Temple wrote to L'Isle from his post abroad:

'The best on't that my heart is so set on my little corner of Sheene that While I keep that, no other disappointment will be very sensible to me'.

He obviously spent his leisure hours planning his garden; in August 1667 he wrote again:

'I am contriving this summer how a succession of cherries may be compassed from May to Michaelmas, and how the riches of Sheen vines may be improved by half a dozen sorts which are not known there, and which I think much beyond any that are . . . I should be very glad to come and plant them myself next season'.

In 1670 Temple, with financial assistance from his father, spent £1,500 improving the house and the garden which even three years earlier had attracted Evelyn's attention. In 1685 Sir William turned his pen towards this favourite pursuit and in *Upon the gardens of Epicurus; or, of Gardening in the Year 1685* wrote with unconcealed pride about the quality of the fruit he was producing at West Sheen:

'For the taste and perfection of what we may esteem the best, I may truly say, that the French, who have eaten my Peaches and Grapes at Sheene, in no very ill year, have generally concluded, that the best are as good as any they have eaten in France, on this side Fountainbleau; and the finest as good as any they have eat in Gascony; I mean those which came from the Stone, and are properly called Peaches . . . Italians have agreed, my white Figs be as good as any of that sort in Italy, which is the earlier kind of White Fig there . . . My Orange-Trees are as large as any I saw when I was young in France, except those of

Sir William Temple by George Vertue after P. Lely, 1679.

Fontainbleau, or what I have seen since in the Low Countries . . .'.

By 1688, the year before Temple retired to Moor Park, Farnham, the diarist visited West Sheen again:

'After dinner we went to see Sir William Temple's . . .;

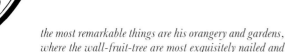

the most remarkable things are his orangery and gardens, where the wall-fruit-tree are most exquisitely nailed and trained, far better than I ever noted'.

In 1724 the author of *The Practical Fruit Gardener*, Stephen Switzer, wrote:

> 'Lord Capel and Sir William Temple were gentlemen, to whom in a real measure we owe that collection of grapes that are now in such great perfection in England and such was the munificence and generosity of that great lover of planting (Sir William Temple) that he distributed them among the nurserymen about London'.

Switzer had already commented favourably on Temple's 'Sheen plum', also known as the red Fotheringham. Another fruit of Temple's which received great praise was his Brussels apricot.

Unfortunately there are no pictures nor plans of Temple's garden, the most detailed representations of the estate being on Rocque's map of 1741-5 and on plans of the 1750s.

Stephen Switzer had linked Temple's name with that of the owner of a garden that lay to the north east of the Charterhouse site. Sir Henry Capel (later Lord Capel of Tewkesbury) (d.1696), a brother of the Earl of Essex, had married the Kew heiress Elizabeth Bennet and moved into the Kew House which stood near to Kew Green and the present Kew Palace; its site is marked by a sundial. The close proximity of the Temple and Capel properties was fortuitous for garden lovers:

> 'I went to my worthy friend Sir Henry Capel, at Kew, . . . it is an old timber house, but his garden has the choicest fruit of any plantation in England, as he is the most industrious and understanding in it.' (Evelyn, 1678).

> 'The two green-houses for oranges and myrtles communicating with the rooms below, are very well contrived. There is a cupola made with pole-work between two elms at the end of the walk, which being covered by plashing the trees to them, is very pretty; for the rest there are too many fir-trees in the garden.' (Evelyn, 1683).

> 'From thence [Temple's] we went to Kew to visit Sir Henry Capel's whose orangerie and myrtilum are most beautiful and perfectly well kept. He was contriving very high palisades of reeds to shade his oranges during the summer and painting those reeds in oil.' (Evelyn 1688).

J. Gibson in his *A short account of several gardens near London* (1691), wrote:

> 'Sir Henry Capell's garden at Kew has curious greens, and is as well kept as any about London. His two lentiscus trees (for which he had paid forty pounds to Versprit) are said to be the best in England, not only of their kind, but of greens. He has four white striped hollies, about four feet above their cases, kept round and regular, which cost him five pounds a tree last year, and six laurustinuses he has, with large round equal heads, which are very flowery and make a fine show...'.

Capel's grand-neice married Samuel Molyneux, Secretary to the Prince of Wales, and they succeeded to Kew House on the death of Lady Capel in 1721.

John Macky wrote in *A Journey through England* (1722-3):

> 'Mr Molyneux ... hath a fine seat here, with excellent Gardens, said to have the best fruit in England'.

In 1730 Frederick, Prince of Wales, took a lease on this property from the Capel Family and commenced the work which was to lay the foundations of the Royal Botanic Gardens. It should be noted, however, that these were not the first notable gardeners to reside at Kew for in the sixteenth century William Turner had a herb garden there; unfortunately no evidence of its actual location has come to light.

The thatched house, which in 1852 became the home of the natural historian Sir Richard Owen (1804-1892), stood to the east of the Sheen Gate of Richmond Park. It was an especial delight to him, and he created a garden there that drew the attention of W. Robinson, the author of *The English Flower Garden* (1883) who wrote:

'Professor Owen's garden – The most attractive gardens are by no means the largest. Indeed, the most beautiful in England are comparatively small ones. Professor Owen's garden is one of the simplest and most unpretending, but withal one of the most charming, in the neighbourhood of London. Many a visitor to Richmond Park enjoys the look of his cottage, as it nestles on the margin of the noble sweep of undulating ground near the Sheen Gate, but it is from the other, or the garden, side that the picture is most beautiful. A lawn, quite unbroken, stretches from near the windows to the boundary; it is fringed with numerous hardy trees. Here and there are masses of flowering shrubs and an odd bed of Lilies, while numerous hardy flowers peep from among the Roses and Rhododendrons. Quite near the house stands a noble specimen of Gleditschia triacanthos, graceful in foliage, stately and picturesque in the highest degree. Its long lower arms stretch far out near the turf, and are laden with their Fern-like leaves, and the whole surface of the tree for 80 feet upwards is broken up in the boldest and most picturesque manner. No tree, except, perhaps, old specimens of the Weeping Beech, displays such an uncontrolled variety of picturesque branching. There is in the main part of the garden only one walk, and this takes one round the whole place, and does not needlessly obtrude itself, as it glides behind the outside of the groups which fringe the sweet little lawn. Instead of this walk coming quite close to the house, it is cut off from it by a deep border of Rhododendrons, intermingled with Lilies and the finer herbaceous plants. These flowers look into the windows. Instead of looking out, as usual, on a bare gravel walk, the eye is arrested by Rhododenrons or Spiraeas, with here and there a Lily, a Foxglove, or a tall Evening Primrose, according to the season. Beyond these, at a distance of 12 feet or so, is a broad, convenient walk. The effect of the border from the other side of the garden is quite charming, the creeper-covered cottage seeming to spring out of a bank of flowers'.

The Rev. R. Owen wrote in his biography:

'The love of his home and of his beautiful garden only grew stronger with his declining years ... he would generally make his way to an extraordinary specimen of a garden-seat, made out of the vertibrae of a whale, which he himself had put up. There are many such curiosities to be seen in that picturesque piece of ground. The skull of a huge crocodile, most of whose teeth are missing ... grins out of a rockery. The plaster cast of a seated Egyptian figure rests on a pedestal at the end of the 'west walk' and a few great bones repose gracefully against a tree in that wooded part of the garden which has always been left entirely to Nature. These little woods are still full of wild flowers which the Professor gathered in his travels on the Continent or his rambles in the country'.

The Duke and Duchess of Fife were near neighbours of Owen; their property being on the opposite side of Sheen Lane and, like his, adjoining the park. The mansion dated back to the seventeenth century and had extensive gardens which were further enlarged by the Duke who seems to have been primarily responsible for the development of the gardens.

The Duke of Fife (1849-1912) had acquired the property in 1880; nine years later he married Louise, the daughter of Edward VII. In that year the *Pall Mall Budget* published the following description:

'The lawn, as level as a billiard-table but of a much prettier colour. It is intersected with paths, in the middle of which is a little fountain with water lilies in the basin. And there are beds of geraniums dotted about, and huge blue and white pots with palms. There is a quaint Japanese summer-house, which looks as if it were made for honeymooning in, with wicker chairs, and Japanese tapestries on the walls. It is only from the lawn that you get anything like a full view of the length of the house, the view from the front being very much hidden by trees. The whole of the grounds are surrounded by a high wall, which is very artfully hidden by greenery of all sorts'.

[The title of the illustration describes the summer house as Chinese].

Four years later the duchess contrived that her brother, Prince George, Duke of York, escort their White Lodge neighbour the Princess Mary of Teck into the garden to look at the frogs in the pond. The Princess was to write *'We walked together afterwards* [after tea] *in the garden and he proposed to me, & I accepted him'.*

In 1905 the estate was sold to a development company and its gradual break up was begun.

CROMWELL HOUSE

Old Cromwell House faced the Lower Richmond Road, and its grounds extended northwards to the Thames. It dated from the sixteenth century, and may have derived its named from Thomas Cromwell, to whom Henry VIII gave the manor in 1536, and whose sister was the wife of Morgan Williams, who had a brewery at Mortlake. Alternatively it may derive from the fact that several of Oliver Cromwell's City friends resided in Mortlake during the Commonwealth period.

Charles Howard, Earl of Nottingham, son of Lord Howard of Effingham of Armada fame, lived here for nearly thirty years, and died here in 1681. In 1689 the house became the home of Edward Colston, the philanthropist whose beneficence is still honoured in Bristol, until his death in 1721. His will makes specific reference to the orange trees, evergreens and statues in his garden. The Aynscombe family were here for over half a century until 1841. The house then fell into neglect, and was demolished in 1858. Its seventeenth century gateway remained *in situ* until 1962, when it was moved a short distance to the west, to form an entrance to a bowling green. The site is now covered by industrial premises.

On the wall overlooking the river was a picturesque and spacious summerhouse or gazebo, with an ogee shaped roof, which features prominently in pictures of the Mortlake riverside over a long period. It was probably demolished at the same time as the house, but its site was identifiable until recent years.

In 1858 James Wigan built a new Cromwell House in the grounds facing the river between Leyden House and Riverside House, and laid out the grounds afresh in relationship to the new house. He was a partner with Charles Phillips in the Mortlake brewery from 1852 to 1877, and here he and his wife brought up their family of thirteen children until his death in 1902. He was greatly respected in Mortlake. After his widow's death in 1918 the estate was purchased by the brewery company. The house was never again occupied, but it was not demolished until 1947.

Gilpin, watercolour artist and landscape gardener, (1758-1843) was the son of Sawrey Gilpin, R.A. animal painter, and nephew of the Rev. William Gilpin, author and illustrator of books on the Picturesque. He was the first President of the Old Watercolour Society in 1804. In his later years he enjoyed a considerable practice as a landscape gardener, and used to claim that he was the only member of his profession. His principal work was in Ireland. In England examples of his work are at Scotney Castle, Kent, and Westonbirt, Gloucestershire.

Another branch of the Gilpin family lived at Palewell, East Sheen, for many years, and it was presumably for this reason that in 1830 William Sawrey Gilpin became the first occupier of 'Painsfield' on the north side of the Upper Richmond Road. He lived there till his death in 1843.

In 1832 he published *Practical Hints for Landscape Gardening with some remarks on Domestic Architecture as connected with Scenery*. The Introduction is dated *'Painsfield, East Sheen, April 7, 1832'*. There was a second edition in 1835. The house survived until 1933, although Paynesfield Avenue had been laid out over the grounds in 1901.

BARN ELMS

The manor of Barnes formed part of the Archbishop of Canterbury's manor of Mortlake (otherwise Wimbledon) but was granted to the Dean and Chapter of St. Paul's before the Conquest, and remained in church ownership until the present century. Barn Elms was the manor house situated at the east of the parish some distance from the church and village, and was let on lease together with park and farm lands extending to over 600 acres to a succession of distinguished leaseholders.

The Wyatt family held the lease during the first half of the sixteenth century, and in 1579 it was acquired by Sir Francis Walsingham. Queen Elizabeth visited her Secretary of State here four times. His daughter Frances married successively Sir Philip Sidney and the Earl of Essex, both of whom occasionally resided here. No descriptions of the Tudor gardens have been traced but tradition has it that a *'rare and beautiful deciduous cedar'* survived into this century, and Gerard mentions planting a phillyrea there for the Earl.

The lake, fed by Beverley Brook which flowed through the estate to join the Thames not far from the manor house, was always a prominent feature and in the seventeenth century there was a formal canal to the west of the house.

In 1639 John Cartwright became the lessee and his family retained their interest until 1750, although the property appears to have been sublet. An advertisement of 1659 listed the orchards, gardens and pleasant walks amongst the estate attractions, and these were much enjoyed during the Restoration when Barn Elms became a popular place for water parties and picnics. Samuel Pepys was a regular visitor who liked to take a boat up the Thames and *'take a turn'* in the grounds:

> *'I walked the length of the Elmes, and with great pleasure saw some gallant ladies and people come with their bottles, and baskets, and chairs, to sup under the trees by the water side, which was mightly pleasant.'* (May 27 1667)

In 1732 Barn Elms became the residence of the banker Richard Hoare, although it was not until 1750 that he took over the Cartwright lease. On his death he was succeeded by his son, also Richard, who lived there all his life. He married his cousin Anne, daughter of Henry Hoare of Stourhead, Wiltshire and it seems probable that he was greatly influenced by the magnificent gardens being created there, for in the 1770s a complete transformation was carried out. In accordance with current taste all formality was abolished, the lake was increased in size to cover 4 acres, it became serpentine and an island was created towards its western end. The seventeenth century canal seems to have been altered during the first Richard's time when it was extended northward under a bridge and then eastward round the ice house mound.

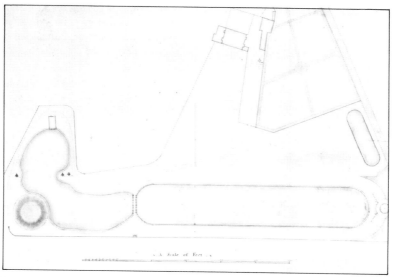

Plan of the lake and canal at Barn Elms, c.1752.
The National Trust, Stourhead.

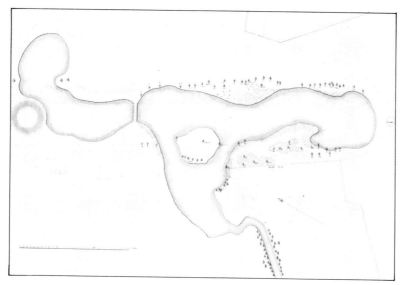

Plan of the lake at Barn Elms after alteration in the 1770s.
The National Trust, Stourhead.

In 1826 when the Hoare family put Barn Elms up for sale the following advertisement appeared:

'*BARNES ELMS*
with its uniformly admired mansion . . . agreeably placed
in the centre of A FINELY WOODED PARK
of ONE HUNDRED AND TWO ACRES OF
RICH LAND.

The pleasure grounds are disposed not merely in the best taste but may be confidently held up as a model whereon the judgement of others may safely confide. Nature has been so bountiful that nothing has been left for art to accomplish. The pleasing diversity of prospect which encompasses this happy retreat, including in one direction the moving scenery of the river, on the other the highly-cultivated plantation, walks and shrubberies clothed with an immensity of choice American and other shrubs. The intermediate space presents

THE ORNAMENTAL LAKE,

occupying 4 acres in a serpentine form, the banks richly clad with stately timber and Portugal laurels – a vista formed of full-grown elms communicates from the mansion to the river. In the centre of this happy concentration of all that can well be conceived, Cowley the poet erected a temple that forms no mean addition to this interesting scene – a little removed are the extensive walled gardens, with a range of 4 hothouses and a conservatory.'

The Hoare family was the last to own the large estate for after their departure it was acquired by the Hammersmith Bridge Company c.1826 for the construction of the southern approach road to the bridge. The estate was divided up and the mansion grounds reduced to 125 acres of garden and park land.

The property passed through the hands of a number of political figures. In 1870 it was acquired by the radical M.P. Henry Davis Pochin who five years later purchased Bodnant in Gwynedd where he initiated the layout of the gardens. It is a coincidence that Barn Elms is thus closely connected with Stourhead and Bodnant, two of the best known National Trust gardens.

Even after 1884 when Barn Elms became the Ranelagh Club particular care seems to have been taken

'to preserve the antique character of the place . . . In the gardens the magnificent trees have been lovingly tended, and such supports as their age demanded have been supplied. The sweeping lawns, so refreshing to the tired Londoner, have not been encroached upon by the small beds and ribbon bordering of modern timers. Flowers grow in profusion. . . a wealth of roses, giant delphiniums, fushcias, cannas, begonias, foliage plants, and many other, including several varieties of water-lilies, may all be enjoyed in their special corners, but are not allowed to disturb the restful harmony of lawns and trees'.

Throughout its existence (the grounds were acquired for playing fields in 1949), the estate was notable for its luxuriant vegetation resulting from the abundance of water. There were outstanding specimens of elms, from which it took its name, planes and cedars of Lebanon, beeches and oaks also flourished. Two centuries ago the pleasure grounds were stated to be:

'laid out with much taste and to have all the advantages of retirement, without being necessarily immured within lofty walls'.

Bird's-eye view of Sudbrook Cottage and garden by William McLaren
from *Garden Open Today* by Beverley Nichols 1963.
Reproduced by permission of Jonathan Cape publishers.

Beverley Nichols purchased Sudbrook Cottage on Ham Common in the Spring of 1958, some months before his sixtieth birthday. The house, actually comprising three cottages built c.1800, stands in just under an acre of ground and is surrounded on three sides by *'high walls of mellow brick'*.

Having spent many years designing and writing about gardens, (his first book on gardening *Down the Garden Path* was published in 1932), he brought an expert's knowledge to creating out of nothing a garden which was to become the delight of the many thousands of visitors who took advantages of its 'open' days. This garden with the aid of his gardener Kenneth Page, within two years was to become a small masterpiece. The formal rectangle was divided into three areas by the judicious planting of trees and shrubs, the serpentine beds of the front section lead the visitor on through a narrow entrance framed by columns surmounted by urns into a larger area at the back. This part too is edged by serpentine beds and has a lily pond as its central feature. Colour was provided by bulbs, perennials and shrubs, but a special and distinctive feature was the thirty foot grey and silver herbacious border which was planted the length of the west wall of the house overflowing *'on to the grey stones of the little terrace,*
and clambering up the old brick walls'.

In *Garden Open Today* (1963) Nichols wrote about the creation of this garden and itemized his three main principles of garden design:

'(1) A garden without water is not a garden at all. Even a back-yard should have a miniature water-lily in a tub.
(2) You double the size of a garden by cutting it in half.
(3) The beauty of a square garden begins with the creation of curves, and the beauty of a circular or irregular garden begins with the creation of squares or rectangles. It is a question of the harmonious blending of the two'.

He continued

'To me, water in a garden has far more than a decorative importance. It is not merely a splash of silver against a green background; it has a mystic quality . . . It beckons a patch of the heavens down to the earth . . . The clouds float at one's feet across the steely surface, the bare branches of the copper beech have the delicate perfection of a Chinese drawing, a bird skims the water, tracing a simple exquisite curve, and round the little statue in the centre is spread a liquid tapestry of purest blue. Here is a province of its own, a place of retreat and solitude, where the world's alarms are far away'.

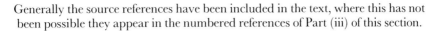
Generally the source references have been included in the text, where this has not been possible they appear in the numbered references of Part (iii) of this section.

(i) General bibliography

BOROUGH OF TWICKENHAM LOCAL HISTORY SOCIETY
Twickenham 1600-1900 – people and places, 1981
(Borough of Twickenham Local History Society Paper 47)

CHERRY, Bridget *and* PEVSNER, Nikolaus
London 2: South, 1983 (The Buildings of England)

COBBETT, R.S.
Memorials of Twickenham, 1872

COLVIN, Howard
A biographical dictionary of British architects 1600-1840, 2nd edition, 1978

EVELYN, John 1620-1706
The Compleat Gard'ner, 1693 Translated from the French of de la Quintinie

EVELYN, John 1620-1706
The diary of John Evelyn, edited by E.S. de Beer. 1955. 6 vols

DEFOE, Daniel 1660-1731
A tour thro' the whole island of Great Britain, divided into circuits or journies . . . 1724-1727

FLEMING, Laurence & GORE, Alan
The English Garden, 1979. Reprinted in paperback 1982

The GENIUS of the place: the English landscape garden, 1620-1820,
edited by John Dixon Hunt and Peter Willis, 1975

GERARD, John 1545-1612
The herball or general historie of plantes, 1597. Republished by Dover Publications
also: *Catalogus arborum, 1596*

HADFIELD, Miles
British gardeners: a biographical dictionary, 1980

HADFIELD, Miles
A history of British gardening 3rd edition, 1979

HARRIS, John
*The Artist and the country house: a history of country house and garden view painting
in Britain 1540-1870*, 1979

IRONSIDE, Edward
The history and antiquities of Twickenham . . . 1797

KEANE, William
*Beauties of Middlesex: being a particular description of the principal seats of the
nobility and gentry in the County of Middlesex . . .1850*

LYSONS, Daniel
*The environs of London: being an historical account of the towns, villages and hamlets
within twelve miles of that capital . . . 1795-6*

MACKY, John
A journey through England, in familiar letters, 1714. 2nd edition, 1722

[PARLIAMENTARY Survey of Twickenham 1649-1650]
Survey of the manour of Twickenham parcell of the Manour of Hampton Court.
Reproduced in *The Book of Twickenham* (Twickenham Local History Collection)

[PYE, J. Henrietta]
A short view of the principal seats and gardens in and about Twickenham, 1760
Various editions followed under a variety of titles

(ii) Maps

GLOVER, Moses
Istelworth Hundred calculated and described by (Moses) *Glover paynter and architecter, 1635*
(His Grace the Duke of Northumberland)

ERSKINE, John 11th Earl of Mar
Skatch of the grounds at Twitinhame from the Earl of Strafford's to Richmond Ferry,
also the Grounds of Ham October 1711 (Scottish Record Office)

ROCQUE, John
An exact survey of the City's of London, Westminster ye Borough of Southwark and
the country near ten miles round begun in 1741 & ended in 1745

SAUTHIER, C.J.
A Map of the Manor of Isleworth – Sion in the County of Middlesex – taken from
an actual survey, corrected & drawn in the year 1786 and 1787
(His Grace the Duke of Northumberland)

(iii) Specific gardens: Bibliography and References

BARN ELMS

BARRETT, C.J.
Barn Elms and the Kit Cat Club now the Ranelagh Club: an historical sketch, 2nd edition, 1889

GARDENERS' CHRONICLE, 1893 April 1 p. 391-92

PEPYS, Samuel
Diary, (1970-1983) 11 vols

CAMBRIDGE HOUSE

CAMBRIDGE, Richard Owen
The Works of Richard Owen, 1803

GARRICK'S VILLA

References
1 **BURLINGTON MAGAZINE**, 1980 Jan
Roubiliac as an architect? The bill for the Warkton monuments by Tessa Murdoch

2 **STROUD, Dorothy**
Capability Brown, 3rd edition (1975)

3 **VICTORIA AND ALBERT MUSEUM**
Rococo. Art and design in Hogarth's England [Exhibition catalogue] 1984

HAM HOUSE

COUNTRY LIFE, 1975 Oct 9
A Thames-side parterre: the restoration of the garden at Ham by G.Jackson-Stops

LANDSCAPE DESIGN, 1976 No. 113, p.26-38

THOMAS, Graham Stuart
Gardens of the National Trust, 1979

HAMPTON COURT HOUSE

HEATH, Gerald
Hampton Court House, 1971
(Borough of Twickenham Local History Society Paper No. 20)
References
1 **COUNTRY LIFE**, 1982 Aug 5
Villa for a mortal miss. Hampton Court House, by Eileen Harris
2 **GARDENERS' MAGAZINE**, 1875 Oct 9
A beautiful conservatory
3 **THE GARDEN**, 1875 July 31
The Conservatory at Hampton Court House

MANOR HOUSE, TWICKENHAM

References
1 Public Record Office, Land Revenue Papers, MPE 1607

MARBLE HILL HOUSE

LEES-MILNE, James
Earls of creation, 1962
References
1 Material for this essay has been drawn from M.P.G.Draper and W.A.Eden,
Marble Hill House and its owners, London 1970, L.Melville, *Lady Suffolk and her circle*,
London 1924 and other sources.
2 I am grateful to Patricia Astley Cooper for bringing this plan to my attention.

MOUNT LEBANON

SIMPSON, D.H.
Twickenham society in Queen Anne's reign from the letters of Isabella Wentworth, 1976
(Borough of Twickenham Local History Paper No.35)
Includes extracts from unpublished letters.

WENTWORTH Papers 1705-1739 edited by J.J.Cartwright. 1883

NEW PARK, PETERSHAM

COUNTRY LIFE, 1982 Sept 30
Richmond's forgotten house: New Park, Petersham by Nicholas de Salis

COUNTRY LIFE, 1965 June 24
A mansion on a damask cloth, by Natalie Rothstein

MOLYNEUX, Samuel
Letter book (Southampton Civic Record Office)

ORLEANS HOUSE

ASTLEY COOPER, Patricia
The history of Orleans House, Twickenham. London Borough of Richmond
upon Thames Arts and Recreation Committee, 1984
Includes detailed bibliography.

References
1 **PLAN** of Mr. Pocock's estate showing Crown Lands, 1808-12
   (Public Record Office)

2 **ASTLEY, John Dugdale**
   Fifty years of my life . . . 1895

POPE'S VILLA

MARBLE HILL HOUSE
Alexander Pope's villa: exhibition catalogue by M.R.Brownell, 1980

MACK, Maynard
Essential articles for the study of Alexander Pope, 1964

POPE, Alexander
The Correspondence . . . edited by George Sherburn, 1956. 5 vols

SERLE, John
*A Plan of Mr Pope's Garden, as it was left at his Death: with a plan and perspective
view of the grotto.* R. Dodsley, 1745 Reprinted 1982

STRAWBERRY HILL

COUNTRY LIFE, 1924 July 5 & 12
Country homes and gardens old and new: Strawberry Hill. 2 pts

ORLEANS HOUSE GALLERY
Horace Walpole and Strawberry Hill [Exhibition catalogue] 1980

WALPOLE, Horace
Yale edition of Horace Walpole's correspondence , 1937-1983. 48 vols

SUDBROOK PARK

COKE, Lady Mary
Letters and journals, 1756-1774 Reprinted 1970. 4 vols

COUNTRY LIFE, 1918 Oct 19
*Country homes and gardens, old and new, Petersham, Surrey, and its houses I.
Sudbrook Park,* by Arthur T. Bolton

COUNTRY LIFE, 1972 July 13
Two dukes and their houses, by Mary Cosh

CUNDALL, H.M.
Sudbrook and its occupants, 1912

SWAINSON'S GARDEN

Reference
1 **LOUDON, J.C.**
Arboretum et Fruticatum Britannicum . . ., 1838. Vol. 1

TWICKENHAM PARK

STRONG, Roy
The renaissance garden in England, 1979

URWIN, Alan
The houses and gardens of Twickenham Park 1227-1805, Oct 1984.
(Borough of Twickenham Local History Society Paper No.54)

URWIN, Alan
Twicknam Park: an outline of the history of Twickenham Park and the St. Margarets Estate from Domesday to the present day, 1965

WEST SHEEN

COUNTRY LIFE, 1974 Jan 17
Statesman into Gardener: Sir William Temple (1628-99), by Ruth Isabel Ross

SURREY ARCHAEOLOGICAL COLLECTIONS, Vol LXXI, 1977
The Charterhouse of Sheen, by John Cloake

WHITTON PARK

COUNTRY LIFE, 1972 July 20
Two dukes and their houses, Part 2: Lord Illay's eccentric building schemes, by Mary Cosh

FOSTER, Peter *and* SIMPSON, D.H.
Whitton Park and Whitton Place. Includes detailed bibliography, 1979
(Borough of Twickenham Local History Society Paper No. 41)

References
1 **KALM, Peter**
 Account of his visit to England on his way to America, 1748.
 Translated by Joseph Lucas, 1892

2 **CLERK, John of Penicuik**
 (Clerk of Penicuik Papers. Scottish Record Office)

(iv) Biobibliography

Places printed in bold type have chapters in the main text. This does not include complete bibliographies for each individual but some standard works are included as suggestions for further reading.

ADAM, Robert (1728-1792)
One of the greatest architects of the eighteenth century, he turned his skills to every aspect of design. Born in Scotland he set up business in 1758 in London where he received the support and patronage of Lord Bute and the Duke of Argyll. It is possible that he designed garden buildings at **Whitton Park** and on **Richmond Hill**.
Beard, Geoffrey *The work of Robert Adam*, 1978

ARGYLL, 2nd DUKE OF
John Campbell (1680-1743)
Grandson of Elizabeth, Countess of Dysart, a successful soldier and victor of Sheriffmuir, he married as his second wife Jane Warburton – a maid of honour of Queen Anne who bore him five daughters. He rebuilt **Sudbrook** in c.1726.
Dickson, Patricia *Red John of the Battles*, 1973

ARGYLL, 3rd DUKE OF
Archibald Campbell (1682-1761)
Younger brother of the 2nd Duke, soldier and lawyer, he was created Earl of Islay 1706. He virtually ruled Scotland under Walpole's ministry. A landscape gardener and arboriculturist of the highest order, many of his trees were transferred to Kew from **Whitton Park**. He was also an important influence at **Marble Hill**.

BACON, Francis (1561-1626)
Writer, lawyer and statesman; **Twickenham Park** was the first of three major gardens he played a part in developing, the others being at Grays Inn and Gormanbury, the family estate. In 1625 he published his essay *Of Gardens*.

BEDFORD, Lucy COUNTESS OF (d.1627)
Lucy Harrington, wife of Edward Russell, 3rd Earl of Bedford acquired **Twickenham Park** from Francis Bacon and created the first of her two major gardens, the second being at Moor Park, Hertfordshire.

BENTLEY, Richard (1698-1782)
Writer, illustrator and friend of Horace Walpole and Thomas Gray, he was a member of the elite groups that acted as advisers and designers at **Strawberry Hill** and **Marble Hill**.

BRADLEY, Richard (c.1688-1732)
Influential horticultural writer. His most notable publications include *Historia Plantae Succulentarum* (1716) and *New Improvements of Planting and Gardening both philosophical and practical* (1st edition 1717)
A general treatise of husbandry and gardening was published in various forms including parts for each month; that for the month of July with its dedication to James Johnstone (q.v.) was published in 1725.

BRIDGEMAN, Charles (c.1680-1738)
Landscape gardener who early in his career worked with London and Wise and later was closely associated with James Gibbs. He worked at **Marble Hill** and possibly **Sudbrook**.
Willis, Peter *Charles Bridgeman and the English landscape garden*, 1977

BROWN, Lancelot 'Capability' (1716-1783)
Landscape gardener and architect, in 1740 went to Stowe and worked with Bridgeman and Kent. A major influence on garden design he became Surveyor at Hampton Court in 1764, prior to this he had worked at **Garrick's Villa**.
Stroud, Dorothy *Capability Brown*, 2nd edition, 1975

BUCCLEUCH, 5th DUKE OF, Walter
Francis Montagu-Douglas-Scott (1806-1884)
One of the country's major landowners, he was responsible for the development of the **Buccleuch House** gardens on the slopes of **Richmond Hill**.

CAMBRIDGE, Richard Owen (1717-1802)
Author, and a major figure in Richmond's literary circle, his house (later known as **Cambridge Park**) had earlier been owned by the Ashe family.

CAPEL, Sir Henry, Baron Capel of Tewkesbury (d.1696)
An amateur gardener of great distinction, he acquired his property at Kew through his marriage to the daughter of Richard Bennet. This garden forms part of the history of the Royal Botanic Gardens, Kew.

CARDIGAN, 5th EARL OF
James Brudenell (1725-1811)
Acquired land, once part of Richmond Wells, in the 1790s and built **Cardigan House** on **Richmond Hill**. He was succeeded there by his wife Elizabeth Waldegrave. He was the brother of George, Duke of Montagu q.v.

CARLTON [or CARLETON]
1st BARON, Henry Boyle (d. 1725)
The second son of Charles Boyle, Earl of Burlington and uncle of Lord Burlington, the architect. He left **Douglas House, Petersham** to the Duchess of Queensberry whom Lady Mary Wortley Montagu believed to be his illegitimate daughter.

CAUS, Salomon de.
French landscape architect and engineer. In England between 1607 and 1613 he worked for Anne of Denmark and her son Henry, Prince of Wales, most notably at Richmond Palace which stood opposite **Twickenham Park**.
Strong, Roy *The Renaissance Garden in England*, 1979

CHAMBERS, Sir William (1726-96)
Architect and landscape designer, he lived at **Whitton Park** and worked extensively at Kew.
Harris, John *Sir William Chambers*, 1970

COLSTON, Edward (1636-1721)
Bristol philanthropist who resided at **Cromwell House**, Mortlake, 1689-1721.

DECKER, Sir Matthew (1679-1749)
Dutch merchant and director of the East India Company, he had a pioneering interest in gardening. His daughter Catherine was the mother of Richard, 7th Viscount Fitzwilliam of Merrion into whose hands **Sir Matthew Decker's** estate devolved.

DYSART, Elizabeth COUNTESS OF and DUCHESS OF LAUDERDALE (d.1698)
Heiress of William Murray, 1st Earl of Dysart from whom she inherited **Ham House**, widow of Sir Lionel Tollemache she married the Duke of Lauderdale in 1672.
Cripps, Doreen *Elizabeth of the sealed knot*, 1975

ESSEX, 2nd EARL OF Robert Devereux (1566-1604)
Married in 1590, Frances, daughter of Sir Francis Walsingham and widow of Sir Philip Sidney was then resident at **Barn Elms**.

GARRICK, David (1717-1779)
Noted actor and playwright who mounted the first Shakespeare festival at Stratford upon Avon. He became a major figure in the local society of the Richmond area and virtual 'squire' at Hampton during his residence at **Garrick's Villa**.
Davies, Thomas *Memoirs of the life of David Garrick, Esq.*, 1780. 2 vols

GAY, John (1685-1732)
Poet and dramatist who came under the patronage of Kitty Queensberry. His play 'Polly' was reputed to have been written in the riverside summerhouse at Petersham.

GIBBS, James (1682-1754)
Scottish architect, most famous for St. Martin-in-the-Fields Church, he worked at **Sudbrook Park** and **Whitton Park** for the Dukes of Argyll and at **Pope's Villa** and **Orleans House**.
Friedman, Terry *James Gibbs*, Sept 1984
Orleans House Gallery *James Gibbs, architect 1682-1754. A man of great fame* [Exhibition catalogue] 1982

HOARE family
Notable banking family whose principal residence was Stourhead in Wiltshire. Sir Richard Hoare (d.1754), Lord Mayor of London in 1745, acquired **Barn Elms**. He married his cousin Anne, second daughter of Henry Hoare of Stourhead. Their grandson Richard Colt Hoare (1758-1838) eventually inherited both properties.

HUDSON, Thomas (1701-1779)
Portrait painter.
Iveagh Bequest *Thomas Hudson . . .* [Bicentenary exhibition catalogue] 1979

JAMES, John (1672-1746)
Architect, and Clerk of Works at Greenwich. Translated *The Theory and Practice of Gardening* by A.J. Dezallier d'Argenville; it was published in 1712 and dedicated to James Johnston, for whom he had built **Orleans House**.

JOHNSTON(E), James (1655-1737)
Secretary of State for Scotland 1692-6, he commissioned John James to design **Orleans House** in 1710.

KENT, William (c.1685-1748)
Architect, painter and landscape designer he enjoyed the patronage of Lord Burlington and the friendship of Pope, for whom he made a drawing of a garden building.
Jourdain, Margaret *The work of William Kent . . .*, 1948
Wilson, Michael *William Kent: an ingenious man*, 1984

KIP, Jan (c.1653-1722)
Dutch artist and engraver, he came to England in 1692. His work included a series of engravings of the great houses of England after the paintings of Leonard Knyff including **New Park, Petersham**. Other views such as **Kneller's house** he both drew and engraved.

KNELLER, Sir Godfrey (1646-1723)
Born in Lubeck, he came to England in 1676 and by 1691 had been appointed Principal Painter to the court. He was knighted in 1692 and created a baronet in 1715. His great house was built at Whitton in 1709.
National Portrait Gallery *Sir Godfrey Kneller* [Catalogue of an exhibition] 1971

LANSDOWNE, 3rd MARQUIS OF
Henry Petty (1780-1863)
The third of three marquises to reside on **Richmond Hill** in **Lansdowne House**. He was the son of the first Marquis who had employed Capability Brown at Bowood.

LANGLEY, Batty (1696-1751)
Writer, artist and gardener, he was the son of a Twickenham gardener. Langley came to prominence as an architectural draughtsman. In 1728 he published *New Principles of Gardening ... after a more Grand and Rural Manner than has been done before.*
This was followed by *Pomona, or the Fruit Garden Illustrated* (1729). Both works were highly influential.

LONDON, George (d.1714)
Nurseryman and landscape designer, he was apprenticed to the royal gardener John Rose. In partnership with Henry Wise (q.v.) he ran the Brompton Park Nurseries which supplied the plants and planned gardens all over England.

MOLYNEUX, Samuel (1689-1728)
Astronomer and private secretary to Frederick, Prince of Wales, he acquired **Sir Henry Capel**'s garden at Kew through his marriage to Capel's great niece Lady Elizabeth Capel. He was himself a keen gardener and enjoyed visiting other peoples, as his letter book in the Southampton Record Office reveals.

MONTAGU, DUKE OF, George Brudenell *afterwards* **Montagu** *and* **4th Earl of Cardigan.** (1712-1790)
He assumed the name Montagu on the death of his father-in-law, John, 2nd Duke of Montagu in 1749. He finally acquired his dukedom in 1766. Montagu acquired two houses on the riverside at Richmond and began the development of the **Terrace Gardens, Richmond Hill**.

OWEN, Sir Richard (1804-1892)
Naturalist and founder and superintendent of the Natural History Museum South Kensington, he was one of the leading scientific figures of the day. One of his close friends in the Richmond area was the market gardener and author R.D. Blackmore.
Owen, Richard *The life of Richard Owen* by his grandson the Rev. Richard Owen. 1894. 2 vols.

PAPWORTH, John Buonarotti (1775-1847)
Architect and landscape architect, he worked at **Orleans House**. He published *Hints on ornamental gardening* in 1823.

POINTER, Vincent (d.1618)
Earliest recorded Twickenham nurseryman, his land was on the **Heatham House** site.
Urwin, A.C.B. *Commercial nurseries and market gardens*, 1982 (Borough of Twickenham Local History Paper No.50, page 4)

POPE, Alexander (1688-1744)
Poet and influential gardener, he resided at the house later known as **Pope's Villa** in Twickenham from 1719.
Ayre, William *Memoirs of the life and writings of Alexander Pope, Esq.*, 1745. 2 vols.
Brownell, Maurice R *Alexander Pope and the arts of Georgian England*, 1978
Dixon, Peter *Alexander Pope*, 1972

QUEENSBERRY, Catherine DUCHESS OF (d.1777)
Catherine Hyde, granddaughter of Lord Rochester married Charles Douglas, 3rd Duke of Queensberry. She inherited **Douglas House, Petersham** from Henry Boyle, Viscount Carlton (q.v.). Kitty Queensberry was one of the leading figures in the literary society of the time and its outspoken champion.
Biddulph, Violet *Kitty, Duchess of Queensberry*, 1935

RADNOR, 4th EARL OF, John Robartes (1686-1757)
Radnor, a bachelor, succeeded his cousin to the title, but not to the majority of the family estates. Towards the end of his life he was on the Secret Service Pension List receiving £800 p.a. Namier says 'most of the men in this list can be described as noblemen living on the dole or on old age pensions *(The Structure of Politics ...)*. Radnor's gardening amused Walpole: 'Lord Radnor ... plants trees to intercept his own prospect that he may cut them down again to make an alteration.' (Letter 8 Nov. 1752).

REPTON, Humphry (1752-1818)
Landscape gardener, he did not take up this profession until the 1780s. He was immediately successful, his designs and notes being presented to clients in red morocco bindings (Red Books), such a volume being produced for **Whitton Park**.
Hyams, Edward *Capability Brown & Humphry Repton*, 1971

Repton, Humphry *Observations on the theory and practice of landscape gardening*, 1803. Reprinted 1981
Red Books of Humphry Repton, edited by Edward Malins. 1978. 4 vols
The Sainsbury Centre for the Visual Arts, *Humphry Repton, Landscape Gardener 1752-1818* [Exhibition Catalogue] 1982
Stroud, Dorothy *Humphrey Repton*, 1962

ROCHESTER, 1st EARL OF
Laurence Hyde (1642-1711)
Brother-in-law of James II, he was resident at **York House**, Twickenham after the departure of his father, the Earl of Clarendon; he then moved to **New Park, Petersham**. This project was adjudicated by Lord Ranelagh.

ROUBILIAC, Louis Francois (1695-1762)
French sculptor who gained the patronage of Edward Walpole. One of his principal works is the statue of Shakespeare made for **Garrick's Villa**.

SLEZER, John Abraham
A German military engineer who went to Scotland in 1669. Between 1671 and 1679 he was employed by the Duke of Lauderdale as surveyor and overseer at Thirlestone Castle and **Ham House**.

SMYTHSON, Robert (c.1536-1614)
A mason who became one of the greatest Elizabethan architects, he came to London five years before his death and made a number of drawings of gardens that interested him such as that at **Twickenham Park**.
Girouard, Mark *Robert Smythson and the Elizabethan country house* 2nd edition, 1983

STRAFFORD, 1st EARL Of
Thomas Wentworth, Baron Raby (1672-1739)
Soldier and diplomat. His riverside residence at Twickenham, entertainingly described in letters from his mother Isabella Wentworth, was later rebuilt and became known as **Mount Lebanon**.

SUFFOLK, Henrietta COUNTESS OF (1681-1767)
Mistress of George II, Henrietta Howard was the daughter of Sir Henry Hobart and wife of Charles Howard, 9th Earl of Suffolk. She was much admired by an influential circle of friends who assisted in the planning of **Marble Hill House**.
Marble Hill House *The Countess of Suffolk and her friends* [Exhibition catalogue] 1966
Melville, Lewis *Lady Suffolk and her circle* 1924

SWAINSON, Isaac (d.1806)
Botanical gardener, **Isaac Swainson's garden** was in Heath Road, Twickenham and is noted in Loudon, J.C. *Arboretum et fruticetum Britannicum* (1838) Vol. 1.

SWIFT, Jonathan (1667-1745)
Dean Swift was a major writer, who early in his career was secretary to **Sir William Temple**. A friend of Pope and a member of the Countess of Suffolk's circle he was one of the contributors to the development of **Marble Hill**. He wrote a charming poem *'Dialogue between Marble Hill and Richmond Lodge'*, Richmond Lodge being the home of George II who had paid for **Marble Hill**.

SWITZER, Stephen (c.1682-1745)
Garden designer, nurseryman and author, Switzer was one of the great influences in the creation of the English style of landscape gardening. Published: *The Nobleman, Gentleman, and Gardener's Recreation*, 1715 *and Ichnographia Rustica*, 1718 and 1742. He visited **West Sheen**.

TATA, Sir Ratan (1871-1918)
An Indian merchant prince and younger son of Jamsetjee Nasarwanji Tata, who pioneered the industrial development of India. Ratan Tata was knighted in 1916. His entry in *Who's Who* described his recreations as travelling, gardening, riding and tennis. His residence in England was **York House**.

TEMPLE, Sir William (1628-1699)
Statesman and author, he created two gardens of considerable renown, the first at **West Sheen**, then second at Moor Park, Surrey. Wrote *Upon the Garden of Epicurus in the year 1685*, 1692.
Faber, Richard *The brave courtier*, 1983

WALPOLE, Horace (1717-1797)
Man of letters and creator of **Strawberry Hill**.
Ketton-Cremer, R.W. *Horace Walpole: a biography* 2nd edition, 1946
Lewis, W.S. *Horace Walpole*, 1961
Walpole, Horace *The Yale edition of . . . correspondence* 1937-1983. 48 vols

WALSINGHAM, Sir Francis (1530?-1590)
Leading figure in Elizabeth's reign, he purchased **Barn Elms** in 1579.

WISE, Henry (1653-1738)
Master Gardener to Queen Anne, Wise had joined George London as a partner in his Brompton Park nursery in 1687. It is claimed that he was responsible for

establishing French garden design in England. In 1699 he published an abridgement of Evelyn's *The Compleat Gard'ner*. He married the daughter of Matthew Bankes. Bankes was probably responsible for him working at **New Park, Petersham**.

WRIGHT, Thomas (1711-1786)
Landscape gardener, architect and astronomer. In 1758 he published his work entitled *Six Original Designs for Grottos* (Universal architecture, Book 2). **Hampton Court House** garden contains examples of his work.

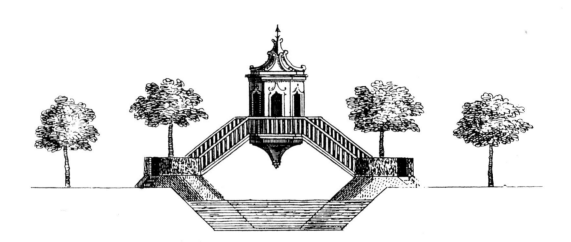

BRITISH MUSEUM
DEPARTMENT
OF PRINTS AND
DRAWINGS 1984